Executive leadership:
A rational approach

Books and Monographs by Albert Ellis, Ph.D.

The American Sexual Tragedy
The Art and Science of Love
The Art of Erotic Seduction (*with Roger O. Conway*)
Brief Psychotherapy in Medical and Health Practice (*with Eliot Abrahms*)
The Case for Sexual Liberty
The Civilized Couple's Guide to Extramarital Adventure
The Encyclopedia of Sexual Behavior (*with Albert Abarbanel*)
The Folklore of Sex
A Garland of Rational Songs
Growth through Reason: Verbatim Cases in Rational-Emotive Therapy
A Guide to Successful Marriage (*with Robert A. Harper*) (*originally titled* Creative Marriage)
Handbook of Rational-Emotive Therapy (*with Russell Grieger*)
How to Live with a Neurotic
How to Live with—and without—Anger
How to Prevent Your Child from Becoming a Neurotic Adult (*with Janet L. Wolfe and Sandra Moseley*) (*paperback edition retitled* How to Raise an Emotionally Healthy, Happy Child)
Humanistic Psychotherapy: The Rational-Emotive Approach
If This Be Sexual Heresy . . .
The Intelligent Woman's Guide to Dating and Mating
Is Objectivism a Religion?
Murder and Assassination (*with John M. Gullo*)
New Developments in Rational-Emotive Therapy
A New Guide to Rational Living (*with Robert A. Harper*)
Nymphomania: A Study of the Oversexed Woman (*with Edward Sagarin*)
Overcoming Procrastination (*with William J. Knaus*)
The Place of Value in the Practice of Psychotherapy
The Psychology of Sex Offenders (*with Ralph Brancale*)
Reason and Emotion in Psychotherapy
The Search for Sexual Enjoyment
The Sensuous Person: Critique and Corrections
Sex and the Liberated Man
Sex Life of the American Woman and the Kinsey Report
Sex, Society, and the Individual (*with A. P. Pillay*)
Sex without Guilt
Suppressed: Seven Key Essays Publishers Dared Not Print

ALBERT ELLIS, Ph.D.

Executive leadership: A rational approach

INSTITUTE FOR RATIONAL LIVING   NEW YORK, NEW YORK

Contents

1 Introduction

What the hell am I doing writing a book for executives? I have been, for almost thirty years now, one of the world's busiest psychotherapists and marriage and family counselors. I have written, during the last two decades, some thirty books and more than three hundred and fifty articles on various aspects of psychology and on sex and love relations. I am a well-known lecturer and panelist, have given hundreds of talks and workshops and have appeared on scores of radio and TV programs in many parts of the United States and a number of foreign countries as well. Then why the devil don't I stick to my own last and let the executives of the world suffer with their ulcers?

Good points. But I have several sound reasons for writing this book. First of all, I *am* an executive. Not a businessman, to be sure; nor a labor union type of executive; nor even a civil service manager. No. But I do run two nonprofit Institutes: one, the Institute for Rational Living, Inc., an adult-education organization which helps people learn and apply the principles of rational living to themselves, their families, and the people with whom they socialize and work; and two, the Institute for Advanced Study in Rational Psychotherapy, which trains therapists and counselors, which operates a moderate-cost consultation center, and which also operates The Living School, a unique private school where normal children not only learn the regular academic subjects but also are steadily taught the elements of emotional education—or how to handle their personal and social problems. So between these two Institutes, I have quite an operation going—one that serves thousands of people and, in the process, spends hundreds of thousands of dollars each year. And, as the *Executive* Director of this scientific and educational combine, I really *execute* quite a number of projects each year.

Secondly, I esteem efficiency. In fact, that has probably always been, and still is, my main goal as a therapist and as a developer of one of the leading psychotherapeutic theories. I think it is incredibly inefficient for human beings to give themselves needless pain by making themselves anxious, depressed, guilty, or hostile; and I spend a great deal of my life fighting this kind of inefficiency. I also think it is incredibly inefficient for human therapists to let their clients give themselves gratuitous grief for such long (and expensive!) periods of time, instead of finding much faster and more elegant ways of helping them. And I therefore spend many hours experimenting with and developing more effective therapy procedures.

Since executives, in particular, are supposed to be concerned with efficiency, since they are usually amazingly inefficient in the handling of their basic emotional hangups, and since they are often the kind of individuals who like rational and effective solutions to problems, I feel particularly drawn to teaching them how to be at least as powerful at handling themselves as they frequently are about handling organizational affairs. To this end, I joined with one of my oldest friends and close psychological associates, Dr. Milton L. Blum, several years ago to do a series of seminars and workshops for executives. We used with them the same kinds of methods that I had been employing for years in rational-emotive psychotherapy and that he had been using in his university teaching, in his outstanding textbooks on industrial psychology, and in his years of firsthand work with executives. Out of this pioneering work which Dr. Blum and I started has developed a long series of other presentations for executives, which he and I have done separately and together, and which we have sometimes done with other of our psychological associates.

A third reason for my writing a book for executives and would-be executives is the large amount of work I do with leaders of business, industry, and government in my psychotherapeutic practice. For people do not merely come to see a therapist because they are upset about their relations with their friends or family. Frequently, they have deep-seated and longstanding vocational or business problems; and I am only too willing to work with them in these areas. When I practiced psychoanalysis a good many years ago, I found the psychoanalytic approach pretty useless in helping people solve their job difficulties. But I have found rational-emotive therapy—which I developed as a therapeutic procedure almost twenty years ago—to be applicable to both the two major areas which Sigmund Freud himself saw as the main fields of human disturbance: namely, work and love. And I enjoy showing a man how he can get along much better with his partner, boss, or employee just as much as I enjoy showing him how he can improve his sex-love relationships. Out of this work which I have done with scores of executives in personal counseling sessions have emerged a good many general ideas and principles. These can be applied by virtually any organizational leader, even (and maybe especially) when he has no serious emotional difficulties but merely wants to conduct his work and get along with his associates more effectively. So this book, in a sense, is one of the most fascinating by-products of my many years of rational-emotive therapeutic experience. Just as rational-emotive psychology can be applied to normal youngsters and their problems, in the course of their regular classroom activities, so can it be applied to normal executives and their problems.

Finally, although I am no great reader of books on the care and feeding of executives, I must say that the few I have read have been in many ways excellent—but have left me absolutely cold. For they generally tell you all the wise, winning, and wonderful things an up-and-coming leader could and should do—*if* he were really capable of doing them. And they completely forget that he practically never is; and that, if he were, he probably wouldn't have much use for these books.

For most executives, these days, are pretty bright and sophisticated. They tend to have good educations, to have had some amount of excellent on-the-job training, to be energetic and ambitious, and to know fairly well exactly where they would like to go. But still they screw up like crazy—even when they "succeed." For you know and I know that Jones has made the presidency of XYX Company at the astounding early age of thirty; that Smith built the PDQ Company's sales from next to nothing to fifteen and a half squidillion dollars a year; and that Johnson started to work at ABC Company twelve years ago as a machinist, and now he's Chairman of the Board and the proud possessor of one wife, two mistresses, and a three-hundred-yard-long swimming pool. But what we often do not realize is that they made innumerable needless asinine errors as they were climbing the success pinnacle; that practically everyone they know hates their guts; and that they are now working on their second ulcer and third nervous breakdown, with the end of that road hardly even in sight.

Why? Because people, including executive people, invariably have screwy traits. They *know* what they would like to do, what they'd better do, and what they have to do if they are to keep out of serious trouble; and then, as often as not, they *don't* do it. Evidence? Well, how about their giving up smoking, losing weight, cutting down on alcohol, being reasonably polite to their mothers-in-law, refraining from telling the head of the firm that he's one of the greatest dunces they've ever met? And what about their being on time to work, returning the book the vice president lent them three months ago, seeing that the budgets for their departments are made up promptly, getting sufficient data to present in the big report to the board of directors? Sure they know that these are the things to do. Sure they know how to do them. Sure they know the severe penalties for doing them sloppily, late, or not at all. Sure they give a damn. But that's all they give.

So most of the books on how to climb the executive ladder are quite good, in their way. Some of them are even excellent. Burger's *Survival in the Executive Jungle*. Drucker's *Managing for Results*. McGregor's *The Human Side of Enterprise*. Carr's *Business as a Game*. Townsend's *Up the Organization*. Great books. Down to earth. Highly readable. No crap. Really worthwhile reading.

But they all have one notable flaw: Who can really *use* them? An angel, yes. A paragon of all virtues, sure. A thoroughly therapized human, perhaps. But a common garden variety businessman? An· ordinary screwed-up college graduate? An up-from-the-lower-classes civil service director? Hell, no! These books—and the hundreds of courses, seminars, lectures, and workshops for executives that abound in the business educational fields —are beautifully designed for the undisturbed, the unupsettable, and the emotionally undestroyed. And where, oh where, are *they*?

Am I saying, then, that the average citizen of the

Western world is ineffably nutty and that therefore he has about as much chance of benefiting from wise words on how to get along with his fellows in industry and commerce (not to mention education and civil service) as he has of flying to Mars on a broomstick? I am.

Am I saying that the bright, often educated, up-and-coming young executive is just as crazy, and in some ways more so, than the average neurotic of modern times? I am.

Am I saying that to be a truly outstanding leader of men you not only would better know what to do and how to do it but also how to *permit yourself,* what with your normal insanity, to do it? I jolly well am!

Furthermore: I am saying that those other books, in spite of their wisdom, essentially evade the issue. For they don't tell you what you *really* would better know how to do to get along beautifully in your executive endeavors. And they pretend that you have all the prerequisites for leadership success, when you are almost certainly lacking the main one: the full acceptance of yourself and clear perception of the crummy reality in which you inevitably reside. Without giving you this kind of knowledge, these books are woefully misleading.

This is not to say that people with the screwiest kind of behavior and frowziest traits do not succeed in the organizational world. Obviously, many of them do! Nor is it to say that graduates of the Harvard School of Business are not provided with a decent amount of salt and ketchup to help them chew up and digest their competitors for top positions in the corporate hierarchy. Often, they clearly are. Knowledge still can be power, and the nuttier you are the more knowledge you'd probably better get. So by all means, if you want to get ahead in the Establishment, go take some know-how courses and seminars in executive management—including the ones conducted by our own Institute for Rational Living in New York and other parts of the country. And go read some of the better books on how to succeed in business by really trying.

But that's not exactly what you'll find in this book. Oh, yes: I'll briefly review the main goals you'd better have and things you'd best do to make those above and below you in the organizational scale see you in a good light and go along with much of what you'd like them to do. As a psychologist, human goals and how to achieve them are one of my main provinces. But as a psychotherapist, I have a still rarer, and in many ways more important, realm: namely, how to help you solve your *problem about having a problem*. And that will be the main—and I think in many ways unique—emphasis of this book.

"You say that I probably have a problem about solving a problem? What kind of drivel is that? What really bothers me is that my associate is great at doing certain things but in many ways is a thoroughgoing horse's ass. Now what can I do about that? *That's* a problem!"

Sure it is. But let's be honest. You're bright. You're competent. You're knowledgeable. You've solved tons of other business problems, including relationship problems. Now why are you making such an issue out of *this* difficulty?

And the answer is, almost invariably, that you do have a problem about your problem. You think that it's *awful* for your boss or associate to be such a horse's ass. That he *shouldn't* be acting the asinine way he is. That you *can't stand* his being that way. That it will be *catastrophic* if he continues to block progress, by acting like a nag's backside, indefinitely.

Let's agree that you're right about him. Let's admit that he's idiotically sabotaging your company's machinery. Let's acknowledge that your life would be much more of a joy if he were not the way he is. You still, as long as you are in any way anxious, depressed, angry, or upset about his behavior, are foolishly creating an *additional* and *needless* problem for yourself: your own upsetness. And whatever you can do about him and his nonsense—and sometimes you can for the time being do very little about it—you most assuredly *can* do something about your nonsense *about* his nonsense. That is what this book, above all other books in the field, is designed to help you do: unloose, change, eliminate your own emotional disturbance. For without your doing something effective about *you,* it is unlikely that you will be able to martial your brains, talents, and knowledge and do something really effective about *him.*

So let's get down to *you.* In many ways you can, and in many you presently cannot, deal adequately with the inanities and insanities of the organizational world. Well, why can't you? What blocks you? What are you doing to sabotage your potential effectiveness? Read on!

A final word of acknowledgment. As noted above, I have worked with executives for years on an individual basis, and have helped many of them to live happier and more productive lives. And, in seminars and workshops,

I have applied my psychological knowledge to groups of executives in general and to specific groups working within an existing organizational framework. The idea for writing this book, however, came from Dr. Milton L. Blum, one of my main co-workers in this field, and a top executive, consultant, and professor of industrial psychology in his own right. Dr. Blum's writings in management have been standard texts for many years; and one of these days he will probably do a book for executives which will epitomize his findings and philosophies of the last quarter of a century. Meanwhile, he has graciously conferred with me on every step toward my producing the present book; and I can honestly say that without his encouragement, suggestions, and editorial collaboration it would never have been written. Not that he is to be held responsible for any part of my specific presentation. But his ideological and emotive support has been one of the main ingredients that have gone into the blood and guts of this volume.

2 The A-B-C's of Rational Sensitivity

Understanding emotional blockings, and doing something effective about unblocking yourself, is as simple as A-B-C. But *simple* doesn't mean *easy!* It's a simple task to diet, to stop smoking, or to give up a long-held superstition. But just try to do one of these things consistently. Simple, yes; but incredibly *hard*.

Still: knowing exactly what to do, in this game of correcting your self-defeating emotionalizing, is at least half the battle won. For otherwise, you become impossibly vague and ineffective. "Sure I'm acting neurotically," you say to yourself. "Now I definitely must stop that!" Or: "Look how angry I got at the Chairman of the Board.

And over such a little thing, too! I must not do that again."

Pious hopes! No matter how clearly you see, or have insight into, your emotional upsets, you are not likely to help yourself appreciably with them unless you specifically, concretely know what you are doing to create them, and how you can persistently uncreate them until they semiautomatically become nonexistent. Acknowledging your problems is fine; resolving to do something about them is even better; but *doing* that something and making it work is quite another thing.

Insight, moreover, can actually be pernicious; since it frequently results in some of the subtlest or grossest self-flagellation known to man. Your observation, "Sure I'm acting neurotically. Now I definitely must stop that!" is in one sense very healthy. You thereby fully admit that you are doing the wrong thing and that you'd better change your behavior. But it also strongly implies: "And if I *don't* stop acting neurotically, now that I clearly see that I am behaving so foolishly, what an idiot I am!"

Similarly: "Look how angry I got at the Chairman of the Board. And over such a little thing, too! I must not do that again." The self-downing implications beneath this admission are (1) "No one else would get *so* angry over such a *little* thing. Therefore, I am an utter nincompoop!" and (2) "If I keep getting angry over such little things, now that I see what a dunce I am in this respect, I shall be a double nincompoop for continuing to do what I see is so asinine!"

All you have to do, when you get insights such as these, is to continue to belabor yourself with them; and, before you know it, not only will you have your original problem—acting neurotically or angering yourself over little things that the Chairman of the Board does—but you'll also have a highly escalated, and sometimes even more deleterious secondary problem: damning yourself for being so insightful and for *still* not changing.

What's the solution? Rational Sensitivity. Which means, as used in this book, becoming exquisitely *sensitized* but not *sensitive*. Or, if you prefer to use more discriminating terms, to teach yourself how to be unusually *sensitive* but not *vulnerable*.

English is a particularly loused-up language, in which the same word frequently has two almost opposite meanings. Thus, the word *need,* as in the sentence, "I need your approval," means (1) "I would very much like you to approve of my behavior, and if you don't I shall be disappointed and may go to some lengths to change that behavior so you will like it better," and (2) "I absolutely must have your approval of my behavior, because if you don't I will take it that you hate *me,* as a total person, and if that is true then I cannot accept myself and have to think of myself as an utter skunk." Obviously, the first meaning of the word *need* here is radically different from the second one. Unless you see the difference between these two meanings, and keep the first one and do something about eliminating the second, you will not merely be sorry and disappointed about someone's not approving of you, but you will be absolutely destroyed.

So with sensitivity. "I am sensitive to your feeling depressed," means (1) "I am perceptive, discerning, and sensitized about your being in a depressed mood. And because I perceive and understand your depression, I can make allowances for your behavior, and perhaps help you to overcome it and to become less depressed." But it also means (2) "I notice that you are depressed and I am vulnerable, highly affectable, and sensitive to your feeling. I can't stand being around you when you are this way, because I quickly become depressed, too. So I hate you and your depression. I feel that I must condemn you for having it, and (at the very least) avoid you when you are that way."

Rational Sensitivity consists of training yourself so that you largely are "sensitive" in the first of these ways and not in the second. It means that you employ your thinking and your emoting so you become more and more sensitized to and perceptive of your own and others' failings. At the same time, you become infinitely less vulnerable, less condemning when you or they display these failings. Rational Sensitivity is tolerance, flexibility, open-mindedness. It is the ability to do your own authentic thing and to let others do theirs without condemning yourself or them when that thing turns out to be foolish, mistaken, or self-defeating.

Rational Sensitivity is the product of rational thinking —of striving for the greatest pleasures and the fewest pains that you can amass in the one life on earth you are certain to live, while not needlessly interfering with the rights of others to enjoy themselves and avoid their pains, and while not demanding that they act exactly the same "right" way you prefer to act. Does this mean that through rational thought you curb your emotions and become less of a feeling and more of a thinking person?

Not by a long shot! Rational thought processes frequently lead to more emoting: to more joy, elation, creativeness, loving, satisfaction in achievement. In fact, the main purpose of rationality is to increase pleasure and decrease displeasure. Reason serves joy; irrationality sabotages it.

So Rational Sensitivity is, of course, rational. But it is also sensation-enhancing, emotion-abetting. It strives for appropriate—meaning joy-producing—rather than inappropriate (joy-sabotaging) emoting. And it does so through helping you *discriminate* between the two kinds of emotion—helping you end up with much more of the former and less of the latter. How? By learning the A-B-C's of emotional unblocking.

You start with C, the *in*appropriate or sabotaging Consequence. The main Consequences that you would like to minimize or eliminate—particularly if you are trying to be a competent or swinging executive—are those which we normally call emotional disturbances, blocks, or symptoms. A typical disturbed Consequence, for example, is inertia, inactivity, or incompetence.

Suppose, at point C, you are sitting on your ass and doing little or nothing to further your executive career. So at C you are checkmated by your own goofing; and, in addition, you are probably castigating yourself for being checkmated.

After finding C, you now look for A—the Activating Events or Activating Experiences that have been occurring in your life before you started to feel checkmated and self-castigating at C. Let us suppose that at point A you met a few serious setbacks—say, the department you head for your organization had a poor year and you were called on the carpet by the Board of Directors and given a hard time about this.

So you now have A, the Activating Events, and C, the miserable emotional Consequences that followed these events. Being human, and therefore inordinately devoted to magical thinking, you normally tell yourself (and everyone else who is kind enough to listen to your woeful tale), "My department had some serious setbacks and the Board of Directors chewed me out for this—and that made me feel inert and self-condemning." And, quite probably, you thoroughly convince yourself and your kind hearers that this was what happened.

Hogwash! Nothing of the kind really occurred; you merely foolishly believe that it did.

Oh, yes, your department *did* have some serious setbacks; and the Board of Directors *did* chew you out. But how could those events, far out in the world, cause you, in the innermost depths of your gut, to feel anything? Where's the hex, the voodoo, by which a departmental failure and a few unkind words by the Board of Directors *made* you feel anything, such as inertia, and *forced* you to berate yourself?

Suppose that I headed your department instead of you, and that I rather than you was bawled out by the Board of Directors for its poor performance that year. Would *I* resort to the same inertia and the identical self-flagellation as you? Let me tell you: I damned well wouldn't.

Or suppose a hundred other department heads like you, all of whom had distinct failures during the year, got roundly criticized by their Boards of Directors just as you did. Would *all* of them feel equally inert and miserable? I doubt it.

Is it really, then, A (the Activating Events) which causes or creates C (your disordered emotional Consequences)? Obviously not. The real culprit—if you think about it—is B: your Belief System (attitudes, values, or philosophies) that you strongly hold about certain noxious Activating Events or Activating Experiences.

And what do you suppose B is, in the instance we're using? Well, B consists of two distinct and widely separated Beliefs. The first is a rational Belief (rB), which goes something like this: "Isn't it unfortunate that my department did so poorly this year? I wish it had done much better. How annoying! And how frustrating it is to be called on the carpet by members of the Board of Directors, especially when they can't even prove that I was responsible for its poor performance. What a drag!"

If you stuck rigorously, unwaveringly, to this rational Belief, you would not get into any emotional trouble with yourself. For if you really believe that it's only unfortunate, annoying, frustrating, and draggy for your department to do poorly and for you to be censured for its workings, you will merely feel sorry, regretful, and irritated about these disadvantageous Activating Events; you will dwell relatively little on your misfortunes; and you will quite probably motivate yourself to do better next time—to take more pains to see that the department improves this year. If so, your emotions—however deep and intense they may be—will be *appropriate* to the Activating Events that preceded them; and they will *appro-*

priately encourage you to do something about these events next time, and try to change them for the better.

Your rational statements to yourself about the noxious stimuli impinging upon you at point A, moreover, are empirically confirmable or validatable. They have observable facts or data to back them. For if I ask you, *"Why* is it unfortunate, annoying, frustrating, and draggy for your department to do poorly and for you to be censured for its poor performance?" you will be able to come up with at least three or four verifiable *reasons* for making this statement. Thus, you may point out that (1) you will not get the raise you wanted; (2) you may be fired as head of the department; (3) the Board of Directors probably won't trust you now with certain other projects you wanted to try; (4) some other executives in your organization may not be eager to cooperate with you as much as they previously did. Since rational statements about unpleasant Activating Events or Experiences invariably take the general form, "I would like to have things *x* way. I am finding them to be, instead, *y* way. Now isn't that too bad!" They are always empirically confirmable. Because your likes can easily be observed and recorded; and your being frustrated in achieving them can also usually be objectively confirmed.

Alas, you are a human! Consequently, in addition to your rational Beliefs (rB's) about the distasteful Activating Events (A's) in your life, you have a strong tendency to slip over into highly irrational Beliefs (iB's). Thus, you will tend to convince yourself something like: "Isn't it *awful* that my department did so poorly this year and that the Board of Directors criticized me about it! I *can't stand* this kind of failure. I'm a pretty *worthless person* for doing so badly; and I'll probably never be able to do well again. If I continue to do so poorly, I should really be punished for my crummy behavior!" It is Beliefs like these that lead to the dismal Consequences (C's) of goofing and inertia, on the one hand, and self-flagellation, on the other. And these feelings and behaviors are, of course, quite *in*appropriate to the Activating Events (A's) in your life, since they will almost certainly cause you to do *worse* in the future and to feel not merely sorrowful and regretful but severely anxious and depressed.

Your irrational Beliefs are crazy not only because they lead to poor results but also because they are completely magical, empirically unconfirmable judgments that have no true relationship to reality. Why? Let's examine each of them and see.

1. "Isn't it *awful* that my department did so poorly this year and that the Board of Directors criticized me about it?" *Awful,* as used in this hypothesis, means two distinct things: (a) "Isn't it very inconvenient, disadvantageous, and painful that I got criticized for my department's doing so poorly?" and (b) "Isn't it *more* than very inconvenient, disadvantageous, and painful that I got criticized?" For, if you are honest with yourself, you can easily see that whenever you use *awful* you do not really mean very inconvenient or even 100 percent inconvenient; you mean *more* than that. Although the first of these points is perfectly sane and validatable—and amounts to the rational Belief which we considered above—the second one is a magical, undefinable, and

unverifiable proposition. For how can anything, really, be *more* than very inconvenient, disadvantageous, and painful? What does the *more* here actually relate to? Does it not give the sentence surplus, mystical meaning, and meaning that truly has no empirical referent? How could it possibly ever be proved—or disproved—that your discomfort in being criticized for your department's poor work is *more* than exceptionally uncomfortable?

Secondly, the proposition that it is awful that your department did so poorly this year that the Board of Directors criticized you about it means (a) "It is obnoxious and displeasing for me to be placed in this position," and (b) "I therefore *should not, must not* be placed in this obnoxious and displeasing position." Well, granted that it is obnoxious, why *shouldn't*, why *mustn't* it be that way? Is there really any law of God or man stating that you *must not* experience obnoxious Activating Events? Is there an ineffable law of the universe that says this just can't be? Of course there isn't! For if you *must not* undergo dissatisfying experiences, then of course you *cannot* undergo them. And you damned well *have* had them! So this is clearly a purely definitional or tautological (and contradictory) hypothesis!

2. "I can't stand this kind of failure." Granted that you don't, and never will, *like* it, why can't you *stand* it? If you really couldn't stand it, then you would obviously fall apart at the seams; and this seems a little unlikely! Since human beings inevitably fail, just because they are human and therefore fallible, they obviously have to be able to stand failure. Otherwise, they would not survive. Not being able to *stand* failure, therefore, is only a defini-

tional construct, which is hardly related to any reality. You can't stand failing because you *think* you can't.

3. "I'm a *pretty worthless person* for doing so badly; and I'll probably never be able to do well again." Although an individual's deeds, acts, performances, and traits can be rated, how can *he* be given any global rating, measurement, or score? For one thing, he is an ever-changing *process*. For another, he is too complex to be given a single rating that would be meaningful. How, specifically, can you legitimately rate yourself as a *worthless person* just because one of your acts—failing at running your department—is below par? And no matter how poorly you have done in this respect, nor how long you keep doing poorly, how could you ever justifiably conclude that you'll *never* be able to do well again? Both human worth and worthlessness are definitional constructs, which are vague, mystical, and unrelatable to empirical reality. To rate an individual's *personhood* or *self* is akin to rating his *soul*. And how can that truly be done?

4. "If I continue to do so poorly, I should really be punished for my crummy behavior." Punishment, as used in this hypothesis, does not merely mean penalization. If you continue to do poorly at anything, you will usually be penalized: meaning, you will not be rewarded for succeeding, will be criticized for failing, will not be able to continue with the project, etc. But punishment means penalization plus *damnation*. It means that just because you have failed, you should be condemned to *specially* suffer on this earth, for presumably countermanding nature's law that you should, you must, succeed. It means

that you are a louse or a crummy person for failing; and
that therefore you *ought* to fail in the future. It means
that you really have no right to live and to continue to be
happy in any way, now that you have failed. But all these
hypotheses, of course, posit avenging gods and demons
(or infrangible laws of nature) for which there is no empirical validity and whose existence could never possibly
be proven or disproven. They are therefore extralogical
or theological hypotheses, and have nothing to do with
human existence except by arbitrary dogma or definition.

For many reasons, then, it can be seen that whenever
you feel exceptionally upset, at point C, you are not
merely responding appropriately and sanely to the Activating Events or Experiences in your life, at point A.
Rather, at point B, your Belief System, you are first
rationally appraising the noxious stimuli that may be occurring at A, and thereby creating an emotional—and
sometimes quite intense—response at C. But you are *also*
irrationally appraising these same stimuli, awfulizing or
catastrophizing about them, and thereby creating a
highly inappropriate, self-defeating emotional reaction at
C. For you are really, whenever you make yourself upset,
a demon-worshiper. Instead of noting, calmly accepting,
and vigorously fighting against the real inconveniences,
disadvantages, and hassles of the world, you are foolishly
and anti-scientifically escalating them into awfulnesses
and horrors.

Rational Sensitivity shows you, explicitly and
efficiently, how to uninvent the devils and goblins you
have nuttily invented and how to replace them with rational philosophies of living. After teaching you the

A-B-C's of personality disturbance, it therapeutically goes on to point D—which consists of Disputing your irrational Beliefs (iB's). Thus, in the illustration we have been using in this chapter, you would at point D ask yourself: (1) "Why is it *awful* that my department did so poorly this year that the Board of Directors criticized me about it?" (2) "Why can't I *stand* this kind of failure?" (3) "Where is the evidence that I'm a pretty *worthless person* for doing so badly and that I'll probably never be able to do well again?" (4) "Who says that if I continue to do so poorly, I should really be punished for my crummy behavior?"

If, according to the theory and practice of Rational Sensitivity, you vigorously and vehemently persist, at point D, in Disputing your irrational Beliefs (iB's) about noxious Activating Events, at point A, then you will almost certainly arrive at point E—the Effects of your Disputing. First of all, you will achieve a cognitive Effect (cE), or a restatement of your original rational Belief in a somewhat more general and more philosophic form. Thus, you will be able to answer your Disputing challenges at point D by saying: (1) "It is *not* awful that my department did so poorly this year that the Board of Directors criticized me about it; it is only very inconvenient. In fact, *all* poor performances and criticisms of this sort are merely quite disadvantageous; and *nothing* is awful, horrible, or catastrophic unless I arbitrarily define it so." (2) "Of course, I can *stand* this kind of failure. I'll never *like* failing but I can certainly gracefully handle it!" (3) "There is not, nor ever really can be, any evidence that I am a worthless person for doing so badly. In fact, there are no worthless people—merely people who behave badly or who are falsely labeled as worthless by others. The fact that I have done badly up to now does not in the least prove, nor ever really can, that I will never be able to do well in the future. The more I learn from my present errors, the fewer I am likely to make later on." (4) "No matter how poorly I continue to do, I never deserve special punishment for my ineffectual behavior. Punishment means damnation; and I, and others, are never to be damned even when we goof and act irresponsibly."

If you persist at getting these cognitive Effects (cE's), at point E, you will then almost certainly get an emotional or behavioral Effect (bE) as well: You will no longer feel like being inert and you will stop feeling inordinately guilty and self-downing about your inertia and the unfortunate Activating Events that preceded it. You will then no longer have an emotional problem about what has happened to you, and you will be much more capable of going back to point A—the fact that your department has failed this year and that you have been roundly criticized by the Board of Directors—and attempt to do anything you can to change it for the better. Thus, you may work harder at your departmental affairs, ask for help in changing some of the organization's policies, try to improve your relations with the members of the Board who are most critical of you, and attempt various other means of helping yourself change the Activating Events at point A.

Rational Sensitivity, then, consists of sensitizing yourself—or becoming wise to—several important things:

That *you,* and no one (no, *no one*) else creates your emotional feelings or Consequences (C).

That no matter how badly others behave, at point A, it is not their Activating behavior but your Beliefs about that behavior which upsets you at point C.

That every time you feel seriously upset—feel, for example, anxious, depressed, guilty, or hostile—you are almost invariably convincing yourself of both a rational and an irrational Belief.

That your rational Belief usually takes the form of: "I don't like this! Isn't it unfortunate that it exists? I wish to hell that I could change it!"

That your irrational Belief generally takes the form of: "How awful that this exists! I can't stand it! It shouldn't exist! I'm a rotten person for allowing it to exist!"

That if you consistently and persistently Dispute, challenge, and question your irrational Belief, it will sooner or later, and often quickly, be minimized or eliminated.

And that if you continue this kind of Disputing, whenever you feel upset, you will finally arrive at a radically different, nondemanding philosophy of life that will thereafter automatically prevent you from frequently upsetting yourself.

The essence of just about all human disturbance, in other words, is demandingness, dictatorialness, grandiosity, two-year-old-ism. People naturally, easily, through biological predisposition as well as through faulty environmental upbringing, devoutly and bigotedly believe that they *need* what they *want,* that they *must have* what they *prefer,* that it is *awful* if they are deprived. They demand (1) that they do perfectly well; (2) that others treat them very lovingly and nicely; and (3) that the world be an exceptionally easy place in which they can live. When they insist on self-perfection they become anxious, depressed, guilty, and overwhelmed with feelings of worthlessness. When they command that others be perfect, they become angry, hostile, sulky, and violent. When they dictate that the world be easy and comfortable, they become goofing, inert, overrebellious, and self-pitying.

Rational Sensitivity sensitizes the individual to his own and to others' puerile demandingness. It shows him what utter folly it is to whine, to cry, to insist that the universe be made especially for him. It teaches him to accept—not to like or encourage, but to realistically accept—whatever grimnesses reality may choose to bring his way; and then, calmly, determinedly, persistently to try to ameliorate them. It shows him how to live empirically and pragmatically, with no delusions but with plenty of goals, values, and ideals.

Rational Sensitivity promotes tolerance, open-mindedness, and flexibility. At bottom, what we call emotional disturbance is something of a high-class name for bigotry, unthinkingness, and rigidity. The disturbed individual narrow-mindedly and moralistically insists on blaming and condemning himself, others, and the world. He is absolutely *sure* that he and/or you is worthless; that things *should* be the way he personally wants them to be; and that it is *awful* if perfect order and certainty do not exist in the universe. The individual who practices Rational Sensitivity, on the other hand, is absolutely sure of nothing; willingly accepts probability and chance; feels that no one, himself or any other, is a worthless *person;* and rigorously and determinedly goes after what he wants without asininely demanding that therefore he must get it.

Rational Sensitivity is also superbly humanistic. It starts and stops with man—and assumes no gods or devils, no superhumans or subhumans. It hypothesizes that although man in one way is not the center of the world nor has he much control (as yet) over many of its processes, he in another way is the very center of his own existence, lives primarily for himself (not for the lower animals or for inorganic matter), and has the ability and the power to run his own life and work creatively for his own happiness. The universe in which he resides essentially doesn't give a shit about him. It probably never will. It is quite impartial and objective, neither for nor against him. Nor does he need it, in any way, to be caring, aiding, and vitally absorbed in his navel.

For this very reason, because the basic atoms of the universe do not give a fig about him, and because he does want to live with little pain and much joy while he lives, man would better be an unashamed hedonist. He *wants* what he wants, even though he may never get some of it; and he *likes* to produce, to create, to lead, to excel, to compete, to win, to make money, to love, to fuck, and to eat—because these are the things he finds intrinsically challenging and enjoyable. These are the goals that enhance his satisfaction and diminish his pain. Rational Sensitivity tries to help him get more—indeed, much more!—of what he wants, and to grow up and accept inevitable frustrations, sorrows, and deprivations.

3 Rational Sensitivity and executive leadership

Rational Sensitivity is both relevant and striving. Many kinds of so-called "sensitivity" procedures today are little more than anxiety-inspired cop-outs. Millions of individuals who are afraid to try for what they really want in life—a good job, a position of leadership, a doctoral degree, or a close, loving relationship—rant and rave against the Establishment, spend a good part of their lives in aimless wanderings, back-to-nature movements, mystical-minded meditation, astrological prognostication, anti-intellectual encounter groups, drug abuse, and various other kinds of disingenuous escapism.

"Suppose," these escapists tell themselves when the going becomes rough at point A, "I really try to succeed at science, education, business, or art, and I turn out to be incompetent or mediocre. Suppose I *never* get to be outstanding at anything I like to do. That would be awful! What a terrible *shnook* I would be!"

Compulsively (and often quite unconsciously) driven by these irrational Beliefs, at point B, they "voluntarily" and "spontaneously" flee from all forms of competitiveness and wind up, at point C, inert, volitionless, and alienated. Rational Sensitivity could save these social and professional dropouts from their defensively chosen fate; but because of their brilliant anti-intellectual rationalizing, they are not too likely to use it.

It is practically made to order, on the other hand, for the leader and the executive. For, almost by definition, such individuals have chosen to remain involved with some kind of Establishment—even when they are devoted to changing it. They are often most aware of the shortcomings of the existing system; and just because of that awareness they give themselves a serious stake in minimizing or eliminating those shortcomings. But, unlike the romantic rebel and the withdrawing hippie, they are organization-minded. They stoutly believe in *organized* efforts for change, and they strive to modify existing structures or to create new ones, so that these efforts will best be fulfilled.

In many significant ways, in fact, the leader and the executive is a born revolutionist. Naturally, he abides to a considerable degree by existing organizational rules: for he knows full well that if he does not, he is not likely to get anywhere near the top of the group, company, or community organization with which he works. And naturally—as is the wont of practically all human beings who get somewhere in life—he easily gets stuck in certain ruts, often forgets some of his youthful ideals, and contributes to nepotism, rigidity, conventionalism, and hardening of the corporate arteries that he himself may theoretically oppose. For the gap between what he ideally desires and the compromises he makes may be deep and serious.

A dedicated organizational leader, however, almost automatically keeps looking for inefficiencies to undo and for efficiencies to construct. He is rarely satisfied to continue indefinitely even the most "successful" and time-honored company policies; for then his work becomes pretty routine and unchallenging. So he looks for what is wrong and he imagines, and out of his imaginative planning tries to create, what is right. Radical, and sometimes drastic, change is almost his second nature; while stick-in-the-mudness is one of his supreme abhorrences. Since radical change is merely another name for revolution, he is in many respects one of the most actively (and not merely theoretically) revolutionary creatures on earth.

The topflight executive, moreover, is essentially logical and rational. At least, he'd better be! For although he is emotive, driving, and behavior-oriented in important ways, he is strong on thinking, imagining, planning, scheming, and theorizing. He does not merely act; he uses his head. His greatest forte, perhaps, is that where some individuals powerfully think, some heavily emote, and some pronouncedly act, he tends to engage in all three of these forms of behavior.

Does this seem to be idealistically overstated? Wouldn't it be more honest to admit that the high-level executive is *mainly* a cognitively oriented planner and a strongly bent mover, and that he really is pretty unemotional, quite mechanical, and not a little inhuman in the way he lives? No, to "admit" this would be dishonest and misleading. The typical executive may seem, on the surface, to be cold and driving; but behind his "coldness" and his "ruthlessness" almost invariably lie some of the strongest emotional urges.

How so? Well, look for a moment at the *man* and not merely at his *works*. *Why* does an executive powerfully execute? Clearly, because he really *wants* to. He immensely wants, prefers, *likes* leading others and running organizations. He greatly *desires* efficiency and success. He passionately *longs* for the attainment of certain organizational goals. He actively *lusts* after various kinds of power. He usually loathes, despises, and *hates* ineffectuality, weakness, disorder, and waste. He knows damned well where he would like to get in life and he *is utterly determined* to get there.

Are these, his wants, likes, desires, longings, lusts, hatreds, and determinations, truly the epitome of disinterest, pure objectivity, and coldness? Like hell they are! Many of his ways and his methodologies may be impressively cool and collected. But what about his intense motivational flames that fan and promote those ways and methods? Are *they* really cool and collected?

The serious-minded executive, then, is naturally rational—for he wants to get things promptly and sanely done—and is also naturally, in the best sense of the term, sensitive. For he is unusually sensitized to the people and the things that are going on around him. He perceives that they are infinitely less than perfect and that they could often be improved radically. For he is also sensitized, in an unutopian way, to the prospects of organizational and human advancement and growth. He not only knows what *is,* but also knows what *could be;* and by sensitively plying between these two important facets of reality, he does his thing to improve poor conditions and to create new and better ones.

Rational Sensitivity logically extends the two main aspects of the developing executive. Being an integral part of the scientific method, and using logico-empirical processes to extend human thought and action, it teaches him to be more effective in setting up viable hypotheses about people and things, to check these hypotheses against available data, and to make conclusions that are internally consistent with the hypotheses and with the data that are found to substantiate them. Being also an integral part of a hedonistic-humanistic approach to the problem of man-in-the-world, it shows the executive (and anyone else who cares to use it) how to become considerably more relevant: that is, more aware of his own purposes and goals in living, more sensitized to the desires and values of others, and more able to successfully harmonize his aims and ideals with those of other human beings.

Rational Sensitivity—like Alfred Adler's Individual Psychology—is concerned with social interest as well as the person's private communications with himself. It fully acknowledges that man has his being-in-the-world; that he practically never is a true hermit; that his personal interests significantly overlap with the interests of his fellows; and that it is becoming increasingly difficult for him to survive, let alone live happily, unless he actively considers the biosocial nature of other persons and the almost infinitely complicated ecological make-up of the environment in which he and they reside. The eighteenth- and nineteenth-century man—and executive— could perhaps be a rugged individualist without too seriously harming himself or his community. But the man of the approaching twenty-first century? Forget it!

Rational Sensitivity is sanely dualistic. It fully acknowledges the quite pleasure-centered, often incredibly selfish, beautifully individualistic bents of the healthy citizen. And it does not snidely condemn or denigrate him for having these bents. For where, without honest individualism, and putting his own interests significantly above those of practically all others, would any individual be? Deep in the soup of cowardly self-sacrifice and ass-licking conventionality.

But don't forget, as Rational Sensitivity doesn't, the other side of the fence of man's existence. Social interest is, in large part, self-interest. No man, as John Donne realistically-prophetically said, is an island. How true this has proven to be since he penned these words some three centuries and a half ago! The executive, in particular, invariably works with other *people*. If his goals and ideals are alien to and at cross purposes with theirs, where are his best-laid plans likely to get? Not very far! And where are they and their purposes likely to end up? Not much farther. He would better get their cooperation, and they his. Whether he likes this fact or not!

Rational Sensitivity—recognizing these realities and their consequences—helps to sensitize you, as an executive, to yourself; to your closest personal associates (such as your wife and children); to your organizational peers, superiors, and subordinates. It offers you an unexcelled key to *humanness:* to understanding the typical, average, infinitely repeatable ways of practically everyone around you. No, it doesn't give any magical "keys to the infinite power of your secret Unconscious Mind." It doesn't put you "in tune with the infinite" or with any special part of the universe which will miraculously help you. It doesn't tell you anything that isn't part of science in general and psychology in particular.

It is rooted, instead, in the basic precepts of rational-emotive therapy which have been widely used and practiced for the last two decades in consultation centers, hospitals, group settings, workshops, schools, and the offices or private practitioners. And these principles, in turn, are based on several decades of psychological experimentation, much of it published during the last decade, which tend to prove with unusual confirmation that human emotions do not originate from nowhere, that they do not arise unheralded in the gut, and that they do not spontaneously flow from early experiences. On the contrary, they are invariably connected with, and often directly stem from, clear-cut perceptions and cognitions; and they can be radically altered, sometimes in an incredibly brief period of time, by changing the conceptions and philosophies in which they are rooted.

Rational Sensitivity uses this psychological knowledge to show you exactly what you are feeling. It thereby places your thoughts, many of which you are partially or totally unaware of, directly at your own disposal; gives you a handle with which to understand and control them; provides you with a way to make them serve your conscious purposes, instead of letting them unwittingly and often compulsively run you and your behavior.

For that is the main secret of executive functioning: efficacious control. The follower and the subordinate can afford to exert little control over his own destiny and activity, and to depend on someone above him, or sometimes his peers, to show him what to do, and even what goals to pursue. The leader and the executive is a dead duck if he is equally uncontrolling. Unless he largely maps out for himself the direction of his pursuits, and unless he vigorously masters some of the most direct pathways to the destinations that he honestly selects, he will probably be indistinguishable from the many who surround him, and will be a "leader" in name only.

The prelude to controlling organizational processes is exerting a large degree of self-regulation. Training and discipline, practice and experimentation—these are the hallmarks of the individual who is ready to innovate and to lead. And each of these characteristics can normally be preceded by the suffix, "self-." For unless you are in good measure self-trained, self-disciplined, self-practiced, and self-experimenting, you are not likely to go too far in executive functioning. The Spartans were well prepared, by early education, for highly disciplined living. But only those Spartans who chose to *self*-perpetuate their childhood training developed into good examples of their unique culture.

Rational Sensitivity, then, prepares you to prepare. You know, as a would-be or an actual executive, precisely what you want to do in many aspects of your life. And you know that you are required, to accomplish these things, to work hard and persistently, to sacrifice willingly many of the things that others spend their lives seeking and gaining, and to continue along the paths of high-level management of others' and your own affairs until, probably, the day of your retirement from active work. You know what you want; and you are willing to think and act for it. Fine! But what are your dire needs that block your strong desires? What are your absolutistic dictates that impede your sincerest wishes? What are your ego hang-ups that sabotage your powerful creative and productive bents?

These are the blocks to which Rational Sensitivity sensitizes you; and by helping you dynamite these stupid and pointless barriers to your greatest degree of executive functioning, it provides you with widened opportunities for love of work and work you love.

4 Enhancing decisiveness

Above all, a competent executive is decisive. He thinks through adequate plans. Then he decisively implements them. While conferring with others and even at times getting in outside consultants, he still takes full responsibility for his own actions and he doesn't whine and wail when they turn out to be mistaken. He is tough without necessarily being rough. He does not hesitate to get rid of ineffectual subordinates, no matter how much he may personally like them; to solidly disagree with the highest official's views, if that is his honest appraisal; to firmly exercise his authority, no matter how unpopular he may at times be for doing so; and to refuse to be swayed by sycophants, in spite of their charm and unwavering support. Although he is flexible enough to change his outlook when new facts and conditions warrant his doing so, he generally has strong convictions and the courage to stand by them in times of stress.

Underdecisiveness is almost always related to one's dire need for approval. Let us consider, as a case in point, Vasil Lating, the sales manager of a hosiery manufacturer. Vasil was thirty-five, had come up from the ranks of salesmen, was smooth-tongued enough to sell a bale of Bibles to the American Atheist Association, ran a fairly successful department with thirty men under him, but could never back up his own decision to fire one of his delinquent subordinates because, "I can't bear thinking of how hard it will be on his wife and family. I know he's not turning in any of the reports that I specifically told him, many times, to get in every Monday; but he's really not a bad egg and I just can't hurt him in any way."

At point C, the emotional Consequence, Vasil's problem is underdecisiveness or weakness. At point A, the Activating Event, he is being defied, week after week, by his nonreporting salesman.

At point rB, Vasil is first telling himself a distinctly rational Belief: "Wouldn't it be unfortunate if I had to fire this man? His wife and his family would suffer by my action; and I wouldn't like them to suffer for his delinquencies. Worse yet, he will probably hate my guts if I fire him—especially when he is really not doing so badly at the selling, but only at turning in the reports. And I wouldn't want him to hate me like that."

If Vasil rigorously stayed with this rational Belief, and refused to go any further than that, he would feel, at C, regretful about his salesman's family suffering; he would feel frustrated about being balked by the salesman; and he would feel displeased at the thought of being hated in case he fired the man. These would be emotions that are all quite appropriate to the unpleasant Activating Events that are occurring in Vasil's life. He would have an annoying situation, but hardly an emotional problem.

But Vasil is *not* stopping at his rational Belief. He is foolishly going on to a highly irrational sequel: namely, "How *awful* that I have to decide whether or not to get rid of this salesman! I can't stand the thought of his hating me in case I let him go. And suppose his wife and children suffer and people find out that they are suffering because I fired him. How terrible that would be, to have them think so poorly of me! On the other hand, if I keep him on and do not make him turn in those reports that everyone else is turning in, he'll be countermanding my authority and making me look like a fool. And how can I possibly live with *that?* Oh, what a terrible dilemma I am in! How will I ever resolve this?"

Because of these highly irrational Beliefs, Vasil is stymied. He gets set to fire the salesman one day, and already has his final notice written—and then he anxiously tears it up. Then he hates himself for tearing it up. Then he hates the salesman for making him hate himself for tearing up the firing slip.

Which means that, in addition to his original indecisiveness, Vasil now has a couple of other needless emotional symptoms: hatred of himself and hatred of the

salesman. His self-loathing is created by another set of irrational Beliefs: "Isn't it awful that I am vacillating like
this! What a dunce I am! I should be making up my mind
and rigorously sticking to it; and I am an utter idiot for
not doing so!" His hatred of the salesman is created by
still a third set of irrational Beliefs: "How can he treat
me like that, the lousy bastard! After all I have done for
him, too! He ought not be acting that way and should
have the decency either to hand in those goddamned reports or else see that he is delinquent and apologetically
resign!"

How could Vasil use Rational Sensitivity to get rid of
his symptoms of indecisiveness, self-hatred, and hostility
toward the salesman? By going on to point D and vigorously Disputing his own irrational Beliefs.

Thus, he could first challenge himself as follows:
"Why is it *awful* that I have to decide whether or not to
get rid of this salesman?" Answer: "It obviously isn't
awful, but just a hassle. Decisions are part of the managerial process; and as long as I'm sales manager, I'll have
to decide whether it's worth keeping a salesman who
clearly won't follow the rules about making out reports
which I lay down."

Question: "Why can't I stand the thought of his hating me in case I let him go?" Answer: "Clearly I can! I
naturally don't *like* for him, or any of the other salesmen,
or practically anyone I know, to hate me—especially
when I haven't done anything reprehensible. It will be
unfair if he hates me after *he* has brought down my cen-
sure on his own head. O.K. So it will be unfair! Who says
that everyone should treat me with total fairness?"

Question: "In what way would it be terrible if his wife and children suffer, if people find out that they are suffering because I fired him, and if they then think poorly of me?" Answer: "In no way. It would be quite sad if I had to fire him and his wife and children consequently suffered; but *I* am not encouraging their sadness, *he* is. And what about the regretfulness of *my* wife and children, and my associates' wives and children, suffering because he is shirking and thereby causing us to be less effective, and probably to make less money than we otherwise might make? What about the trouble he is directly and indirectly giving me and my family—don't those pains count, too? I certainly won't like it if people find out I've fired him and detest me because I've presumably made his loved ones suffer. But what are they really going to *do* to me if they dislike me—burn down my house or put a bullet through me? A sales manager, for one reason or another, has to be disliked by various people. Tough shit!"

Question: "Suppose I keep on avoiding the issue and do not make him turn in those reports that everyone else is turning in, why will I look like a fool? And if I do, why can't I live with that?" Answer: "There is no evidence that I'll look like a fool, in those conditions. On the contrary, there is some evidence that I will if I keep letting him get away with things like not making out the reports and this comes to the attention of my superiors or subordinates. But why, anyway, does *looking* like a fool *make* me one? It's too bad if I seem like a horse's ass to those who know how I am letting him get away with things; and I certainly won't like their viewing me in that manner. But I can make myself feel like a person who has done a foolish *act* rather than a person who is a *fool* for doing that act. The only 'fool' is one who thinks he is; and I'll be damned if I let myself think in that foolish manner!"

Question: "What makes me think that the dilemma I am in is so terrible?" Answer: "True, it has no perfect solution. If I keep on this salesman, I am acting weakly and will have to pay various consequences for my weak behavior. If I let him go, I am acting strongly but will still have to pay certain consequences for my strong behavior. So whatever I do, I'm to some degree screwed. O.K. So I'm screwed! Who said that human beings, such as myself, *should* not be screwed? I did. Well, when am I going to stop saying that nonsense and accept reality? Pronto!"

So Vasil could work—and I mean actively *work*—against his indecisiveness about firing the salesman. At the same time—or even prior to this—he could also work at giving up his hatred of himself and of this man who is helping cause his dilemma. How? By Disputing, at point D again, his irrational Beliefs about himself and about this man. Thus:

Question: "What makes it *awful* for me to be vacillating like this?" Response: "Nothing makes it awful. It's a blasted nuisance for me to keep shilly-shallying, and not coming to any definite decision about getting rid of him. But that's *all* it can possibly be: a blasted nuisance. It's never *more* than a nuisance; and there's no reason in the world why I *shouldn't* be annoying myself like this. If I am, I am! Now, how the devil shall I stop bothering myself and make a decision with a minimum of further vacillation?"

Question: "Where is the evidence that I am a dunce or an idiot for not making up my mind and rigorously sticking to it? Why *should* I?" Response: "There is considerable evidence that I am acting in a stupid and idiotic manner, in this respect; but that hardly makes *me,* a total and ongoing person, a dunce or an idiot. Just about all human beings act duncelike and idiotic at times; and are they *all* complete dunces? There is no reason, moreover, why I *should* make up my mind and rigorously stick to it, though there are several reasons why *it would be much better* if I did. Now let me, for *those* reasons, make a decision and go through with it; and let me leave all *shoulds* and *musts* to God and the Devil—who, so far, haven't done a very good job, in spite of their presumably high positions in the order of things, precisely defining them and seeing that they are inexorably carried out."

Finally, in regard to his hating the salesman he is considering firing, Vasil could sanely ask himself these Disputing questions:

Question: "Why can't he treat me like that—refusing to do his reports and thus placing me in a dilemma about firing him? And why is he a bastard if he does?" Reply: "He *can* treat me like that. In fact, it seems to be one of the easiest things of which he is capable! Not only can he; he clearly has no trouble doing so. And he is no more a bastard for doing this shirking act than I am a nincompoop for vacillating about firing him. Like me, he is an inordinately fallible individual. Well, fancy that!—we're both members of the human race!"

Question: "Why ought he not, after all I have done for him, behave the way he is behaving? And why should he have the decency either to hand in those goddamned reports or else see that he is delinquent and apologetically hand in his resignation?" Reply: "No reason whatever! Even though I may have done many things for him, he has the prerogative, as a human being, to return my favors with unkindnesses. I think he's wrong in not rewarding me for my consideration of him; but, like all people, he has a right to be wrong, and I'd better realistically expect that he often will be. It would be great if he had the decency to hand in those reports or apologize for his delinquencies; but he doesn't *have* to do what would be great. In fact, he doesn't have to do *anything* I would like him to do. Ever!"

So much for Disputing, at point D. If Vasil proceeded in this manner, he would be likely to end up with a few new cognitive Effects (cE) or philosophies:

1. Indecisiveness and vacillation are foolish and needless. But they are never awful or catastrophic.

2. If my subordinates or associates hate me for being decisive, that's tough!

3. I can easily do foolish acts, but only a magician can turn *me* into a fool.

4. Executives get damned if they do and damned if they don't get rid of ineffectual people. Either I accept that fact or join the foreign legion.

5. There are, as far as can be determined scientifi-cally, no absolute shoulds, oughts, or musts in the uni-verse. And if there were, it would probably be deadly!

6. People are fallible because people are people. Maybe when I get to Heaven I will work with a bunch of angels. But not till then!

How about overdecisiveness? Can that sometimes be a problem, too?

Definitely! The person who is overdecisive makes choices, all right, but tends to make them too quickly and rashly. There are distinct advantages about this kind of behavior: It saves time, is clear and precise, lets other members of the organization know where he stands, and is often quite efficient. But what a risk! Especially when the overdecisive individual has important decisions to make, votes to spend huge sums of money in the course of making them, involves the employment or nonemploy-ment of many workers, and has in his power the future growth and development of his entire plant.

How can you stop making overimpulsive decisions? By checking, as usual, the irrational Beliefs that you are cre-ating to compel and impel them. Let's look again at the A-B-C's of the situation.

At point A, there is an Activating Event calling for a decision—which could be the same kind of event we just hypothesized in regard to underdecisiveness. Let's as-sume that you are sales manager of a firm and one of your very best salesmen is disregarding your clear-cut in-structions to hand in detailed sales reports at the end of every week. This time, instead of endlessly dillydallying about whether or not to fire him, you give him very little chance to correct his errant ways and you quickly can him. The president of your company, who knows how good the man is (and who has never been enthusiastic about your report-demanding procedures anyway), takes a dim view of your action and demands: "How come? I can understand that you might let one of our ordinary salesmen go when he shirked on his report-making. But let's face it: This man was exceptional. No one we ever had did so well. Now, do you really think firing him that quickly, without even giving him a chance to reform his ways, was justified?"

"Well," you say to the president, "I really don't know. Maybe I was a bit hasty." But what you say to yourself is a lot stronger: "Shit!—I certainly goofed that time. Why *did* I fire him so rapidly, without giving him a chance to change? There goes my dratted overimpulsiveness again!"

So at A you had to make some kind of decision; and at C you did—overimpulsively and stupidly. Why?

Because, as ever, of B. First, you told yourself some sort of rational Belief (rB). Probably: "What a pain! Just as everything was going so well in sales, this joker has to start disobeying my rules and acting as if he owned the lousy firm. Now I have to decide whether to let him go or not. Christ! And he just happens to be my best man, too. What putrid luck!"

But this rational Belief, as is invariably the case, only caused you to feel sorry, regretful, annoyed. Had you stopped right there, the chances are that you would have got after the man again, even three or four more times, and given him every reasonable chance to change his ways before you fired him.

But you didn't. You got pissed off, instead, and told the personnel department to give him notice immediately. Then, when he tried to talk to you, to admit that he had been delinquent, and to ask for one more chance, you curtly cut him off and rigidly stuck to your guns. You knew darned well that you'd have to account to the president for letting him go; but you simply cursed him under your breath, even more, for *that* indignity he had caused you, and you practically threw him out of your office.

So what did you convince yourself at iB—your irrational Belief? Several things:

1. "He can't do that to me! Imagine—after I've already told him three times about those late reports, he not only is late again with this one, but it looks like he has no intention of *ever* turning it in. And with no excuse or apology, either! How can he do this to me?"

2. "Boy, what a slob I'll be, to him and to everyone else in the firm, if I let him get away with this! What kind of a sales manager am I, if I don't put him in his place? I'll be the laughing stock of the whole firm—and he'll be perfectly right in not paying any attention to a *schlemiel* like me!"

3. "Why wait a minute longer to get rid of him? I can't even stand to face the bastard, knowing he knows I'm letting him take advantage of me. I'll bet he planned the whole thing—just to embarrass me with the president. What a slimy skunk he is! He's no doubt gloating

about the position he's placed me in. Well, I'll fix his wagon, if it's the last thing I do!"

In other words, at point iB—your irrational Belief System—you insanely concluded that this salesman *shouldn't* be the way he is; that he has made a *perfect monkey* out of you; and that as a result of his crummy behavior you absolutely *cannot stand* him a minute longer. Because of your anger, self-deprecation, and low frustration tolerance you have literally driven yourself to make a hasty, impulsive, ill-chosen decision about firing the man; and you have thereby impaired your own executive ability and position.

The man's *behavior,* then, is not the real issue—however execrable it may be. You are roundly and totally condemning *him,* and not merely his *acts.* And ironically, and with real poetic justice, you are also castigating yourself, your being, your whole existence, just because your associates may notice that he has defied you, may see that you have not yet figured out any foolproof way of handling him, and may look down on you for your ineptness. Agreeing with what you imagine will be their assessment (actually, they may come to quite different conclusions about his actions and your reactions), you have adopted the mantle of general shithood, and have demeaned your *self* for your unsuccessful *deeds.* Finally, because you have falsely concluded that you cannot for a minute more stand the sight of this epitome of iniquity—the person who above all others reminds you of your horrible ineptitude—you have summarily rid yourself (and your company) of his presence, and have thereby brought on your head the displeasure of your highest executive officer.

The solution to your practical problem may be fairly close at hand. For you may soon pacify the president, hire another crackerjack salesman, change your rules about weekly reports, or otherwise correct the bad situation that has just been created by your rashly getting rid of this salesman. But your *emotional* problem distinctly remains.

For what are you going to do and how are you going to feel the next time a similar situation arises? If you still basically believe the nutty ideas that got you into this hassle, why should you not assail yourself with them again—and again—and again? What makes you think this kind of rash decision won't recur? So solving the objective problem is not enough; what are you going to do about changing your rashness?

The answer—if you are to employ the A-B-C's of Rational Sensitivity is: on to Disputing, at point D! Why don't you take another, and closer, look at your irrational Beliefs and vigorously question and challenge them? For example:

Question: *"Why* can't he do that to me?" Answer: "With no trouble whatever, he can! No matter how many times I've told him to get those reports in earlier, there is no reason why *that* should make him do them on time, or make him have any intention of turning them in at all. So, in this respect, he is an arrant goofer, and a nonapologetic goofer at that. Considering what humans are, and considering how good salesmen (in particular) often try to get away with murder, that's hardly surprising! Maybe I'd better grow up and accept him as he is, since his advantages seem to far outweigh his limitations."

Question: "How does his getting away with not handing in the reports I requested actually make me a slob?" Answer: "It doesn't. At worst, it makes me a person who in this one respect is letting him get away with something. All right—so in some ways I'm weak. Or—if I look at it a little differently—maybe I'm strong enough to take disrespect from one of my salesmen when it's to my advantage, considering how good a man he is in other ways, to disregard some of his shirking. On the other hand, what if I sometimes act weakly or others see me as being weak? Does that really make me a thoroughgoing weakling, a slob? Hardly! It merely makes me a human being with weaknesses. Which is too bad, but hardly awful."

Question: "Why can't I stand to face the bastard?" Answer: "I can! I may never like facing him, for he is a partially disruptive force in my department, and I'm hardly going to applaud some of his behavior. But I *can* stand what I don't like. Even if he deliberately engineered this whole thing, in order to embarrass me with the president—which I doubt, because it would be a foolish thing for him to do and there is no evidence that that is why he did it—he has every right to think the way he does and to do things for his own peculiar motives. And there's no use in my trying to fix his wagon if, in the process, I do myself in. I'd better mainly take care of me, and forget about spending my time and energy in fixing him."

If you persist at this kind of Disputing and at thinking through the logical and data-backed answers to your challenges, the chances are that you will at least temporarily come up with quite a different philosophy toward situations like this one to which you rashly overreacted. And, after meeting these situations with similar challenges on several occasions, you will finally deeply hold and automatically adhere to the new philosophy.

Thus, eventually you can unconsciously (as well as consciously) react with this kind of central view: "Even people who do excellently in one respect frequently do badly in another. Just because a salesman is on the ball in selling is no reason to suppose that he will be equally responsible and adept at promptly turning in sales reports. The more I overreact to poor behavior on the part of one of the men under me, the more he is likely to become resentful and to deliberately buck me. Considering that this is the way innumerable (though not necessarily all) people are, why can't I calmly accept this fact, and even use it to my advantage? And if I hesitate or act weakly in a situation like this, why can't I accept my limitations and convince myself that it is not horrible to have other people, including my salesman or my superiors, know about them? I can—and I'm going to!"

At this point, if you persist, you will tend to lose your *compulsion* to make hasty, overemotional decisions; and you will be inclined more slowly, and with some amount of careful thought, to decide issues on the basis of the greatest all-around advantage for you and your organization and not on the basis of how seriously your "ego," or your ratings of yourself, will be affected. More on this important "ego" matter later in this book. For if you really solve the basic problem of "ego" and "self-worth," you will not only be far ahead of the game in terms of executive efficiency but will become invulnerable to most of the personal slights and "insults" that are likely to come your way in other important areas of your life.

5 *Increasing efficient concentration*

The most important element in executive competence is probably sustained focusing or concentration. Anne Roe, one of our leading psychologists, did a noted study of outstanding scientists some years ago, to discover exactly why they were leaders in their field, when many other equally brilliant and well-trained scientists were not. She found that they almost all exhibited one major trait: They genuinely liked what they were doing more than they enjoyed anything else in the world. Therefore they concentrated most of their effort on their work and relatively little on many other aspects of living upon which the average scientist spends large amounts of time and energy.

Much the same thing has been found in studies of organizational leaders. The effective executive is almost always a person who concentrates beautifully, much of the time, on his work; and who, when a particular problem or project comes along, intensely focuses on many aspects of it in a determined, never-say-die attempt to complete it successfully.

Take, first, the general goal of being a topflight organizational head. Are you really *determined* to achieve this goal? Well, if you want to be successful at it, you'd darned well better be! Of course, to be so monolithically intent on getting to the top of the organizational ladder that you'd commit any act, including murder, to get there is going too far. But not much! For ruthless determination to get what you want is perhaps three-quarters of the battle won; and the harder you drive to succeed in your executive goals, the greater are your chances of fulfilling them.

To whom, for example, are your main loyalties to be devoted? The company? Your superiors? Your subordinates? Not by any means! The answer, of course, is *you*. You pick the company, and choose to stay with it, because *you* think you can get somewhere, and perhaps pretty fast, in it. If not, get the hell out. Pick a better company for your purposes. Don't let sentiment, habit, or the hassles of change stand in your way.

Similarly with raises, with taking on new responsibilities, with getting along with this associate or wisely avoiding that one. What do *you* want to achieve? How can *you* achieve this end? Where do *you*, temporarily and ultimately, want to get? Sure you can have other goals—like developing real friendships with some of your associates; like making your organization the best of its type in the world; like using the influence and power of your firm to help the country's economy or to encourage world change. But let's face it: These are *your* goals and ideals. You still basically pursue them because *you* want to do so. And the better and more powerful an executive you become, the more likely you are to achieve them. So company interest and friendship-within-the-company interest are fine and rewarding. But are they really *your* primary concern?

Once you decide, your personal aims will be furthered by staying with and working in a given organizational setup, you'd better actively concentrate on how to get the most work done, with maximum effectiveness, in the least period of time. For whether you work in business or industry, for government or a nonprofit corporation, in manufacturing or in some service-oriented field, manpower (especially these days!) is expensive. What can you, therefore, do to efficiently use your own and others' time, to cut down the cost per unit of whatever your organization turns out, and to keep things smoothly rolling in spite of the innumerable ordinary and special hazards that are likely to interfere?

Some general rules in this respect: Try to focus on the *most important* things to be done, by you and others, for your firm's main purposes. Check on routines that have become formally established just because they once worked but may now have little use and involve much waste. Avoid trivia—including the perfect performance of inconsequential tasks. Concentrate on first things first:

the goals that have definite deadlines and on whose successful achievement several other subsequent goals are
likely to depend. Face the fact that, for all your energy
and fervor, you are one limited human being, with only a
dozen or so hours a day at your working disposal, and
that you can't possibly do everything you'd like to accomplish considering these limitations.

Watch your—and, sometimes, others'—social life in
the office. Time that is originally well budgeted can easily
be dissipated in pleasant chitchat. Are you really cement-
ing your good relations with your superior when you visit
his office for half an hour at a time to discuss your golf
games? Are you not indulging yourself—and him—un-
necessarily and practically assuring that you both will
have to stay late that evening or abandon some desirable
tasks?

What about the special reports you demand from your
subordinates? Are they truly desirable or necessary?
What about the meetings and conferences you keep calling or unthinkingly attending? Do they aid or impede organizational progress? Yes, it is fascinating for you to
keep taking on new projects and to diversify your doings
in a number of ways. But is that, realistically, the thing to
do? Is it likely to get you, your company, or anyone you
really care about anywhere?

Some of these things you haven't quite realized, and
now that they are being brought to your attention you
will see and start heeding. But some of them you have
seen for quite a while—and you still are far from
carrying them out. O.K.: why? What stops you from
efficient concentration? The answer is: *You* stop you. At

point A, you know perfectly well what to do. And at point C, you don't do it. What's B? What's your interfering bullshit at B?

The main bullshit, probably, is your low frustration tolerance or short-range hedonism. Sure you know it's wise to avoid trivia, to focus on first things first, and to stop wasting time oversocializing with your boss, your peers, and even your subordinates. But knowledge isn't the same thing as action. Instead of sticking with your rational Beliefs, at point B, you lap over to irrationalities like these: "I know it's right to avoid trivia and to focus on more important affairs. But it's so easy to do otherwise! And it's so hard not to! In fact it's *too* hard. I'm just not made that way. I just *can't* keep reminding myself that I'd better limit my golf conversations with my boss to a few minutes at a time; this wouldn't be *me*. I've *got to* be able to be myself, and spontaneously go on, in these situations; else life is hardly worth living, and what am I working for, anyway? Damn it, why should I *have* to be so careful about budgeting my time?"

These are irrationalities because they do not particularly accord with the executive way of life that you have chosen. After all, no one *forced* you to become a leader in your organization; and no one is *insisting* that you make it to the top of the hierarchy. Even if your wife and family, your friends, and your sainted mother and father all vehemently want you to make a million dollars or become the president of the United States, they can't *make you* accede to their goals. Only you can decide where you are determined to get in life. But once you have decided and you have made getting to or close to the top your main purpose in remaining with a given group or organization, then you'd better take the consequences of your own decision; and one of the chief consequences is concentrated effort.

So if, in accordance with the schema of Rational Sensitivity, you want to move on to point D, and Dispute your low frustration tolerance and short-range hedonism that is interfering with your sensibly focusing on executive advancement, you can challenge yourself along these lines: "Naturally, it's easy for me to focus on trivia and thereby to consume time and energy that I could otherwise spend in concentrating on more important organizational and personal goals. Sure it's hard not to do this. But why is it *too* hard? If it really were too difficult for me to do this, then I'd better give up my executive duties, or at least be satisfied to stay where I am, and resign myself to my limitations. For if I can't do better, then I just can't; and how can I do better than I am possibly able to do?

"But *is* it really *too* hard; or isn't it just *hard?* And why *can't* I keep reminding myself that I'd better limit my golf conversations with my boss to a few minutes at a time? I know, so far, that I *don't* and *won't*. But does that mean I *can't?*

"As for concentrating on important business affairs rather than on pleasant chitchat not being *me,* what kind of crap am I handing myself? Is it *me* to get up in the morning to get to work on time, even when I feel like sleeping another couple of hours? Is it *me* to avoid telling my wife that the new dress she likes so much is a holy horror, when I really think it is? Of course it's *me!* It's *me* to do all kinds of unpleasant things now in order to avoid unpleasant complications or to enjoy myself more in the future. That's one of the most basic aspects of *me:* to put off present pleasure for future gain. Why am I idiotically trying to convince myself, then, that limiting my golf conversations with my boss would not truly be *me?* Who would it be—the man in the moon?

"Do I really *have* to be 'myself' at all times and spontaneously go on in these easy situations, such as having prolonged talks about golf with my boss, just because I often *like* to do this kind of thing? Would my life, as a whole, really be hardly worth living if I gave up a few more of these easily available pleasures—and thereby tried to bring about more ultimate gain? Or wouldn't it, actually, be somewhat *more* worth living, more productive of long-run advantages? Of course, I don't *have* to be so careful about budgeting my time at the office, and I *could* continue to be careless about it. But isn't more thoughtful budgeting worth the effort? And is the non-budgeting likely to bring about as much pleasure as I assume it will bring? What's truly more advantageous for the *me* that I'm presumably protecting with my short-range hedonistic view of things?"

Allied to your refusing to focus on first things first in your work is the concept (which unfortunately most human beings are prone to devise) of maintaining *false* integrity. For you may agree it is wise and sane to ask yourself what you really want in life from your daily endeavors, and it is worth dealing diplomatically with your associates in order to insure certain gains (such as job success). But if you push this question too far, you may conclude that it is crazy to do something you don't want to do spontaneously and that if you do what you "feel" unpleasantly about, you will sell your soul to mammon or the devil and will have nothing left of *yourself*. Thus, you will conclude that, because you spontaneously *want* lengthy golf discussions with your boss, in order to maintain your honest integrity and your authentic being, you simply must do what you want to do about these golf conversations and the devil (and your firm) take the hindmost!

The reason this so-called integrity that you are thereby maintaining is false is that you are often cutting off your nose to spite your face. For however much both you and your boss enjoy the golf conversations, and however much you'd rather talk about (or, for that matter, play) golf instead of sticking to business affairs, you *also* desire pretty strongly to get promoted, to make more money, to help build up your firm, to get in the good graces of your boss's bosses, and to do many other things besides converse about golf. Consequently, your *real* integrity consists of divining, after a considerable amount of thought, not merely what you want to do *right now* or what you want to do *in itself* but what you want to do mainly, on the whole, and in the context of your entire life. And if that thing is primarily to be an efficient, up-and-coming executive, then you are very falsely "maintaining your integrity" by insisting on doing, right here and now, an enjoyable but *secondary* thing: namely, endlessly conversing about golf. In these circumstances, your *real* integrity would be sustained by your *not* talking rather than by your deliberately and willfully talking about golf, in spite of your honest enjoyment in doing so.

If this is so, then your Disputing your own irrational Beliefs could continue as follows:

"It would be great if I could keep discussing golf for a half hour a day or more with my boss. Both he and I truly enjoy this; and we can often easily get more wrapped up in that kind of discourse than we can in purely business affairs. But I (and perhaps he, too) hardly like the *consequences* of such talks—the fact that before we know it the day goes by and many important things are hardly attended to. Therefore, if I am to maintain my own integrity, I'll certainly keep talking to him about golf, from time to time. But I'll *also* keep in mind my other, and often more significant, goals: to be an effective executive and to show my associates, including him, that I am in this category. My integrity involves going after what I *most* want, and not only what I want, in life. Now let me, not just as an executive, but as the executive of my *own* existence, give some serious thought and action to *that* goal!"

If you persist at this kind of Disputing, at point D, of your irrational Beliefs that keep producing your low frustration tolerance and your sense of false integrity, you ultimately tend to arrive at a fairly consistent and automatic new cognitive Effect or philosophy of life and work. This takes the form of: "So being an efficient executive is often hard and involves my sacrificing a number of immediate gratifications. Why *shouldn't* that be so? Nobody promised me an organizational rose garden! And if I want what *I* want, I'd better be prepared to pay the piper. I certainly might *like* it to be easier. But that's not the way it is. Tough!"

6 *Improving relations with others*

As every personnel department knows when it comes to hiring or promoting an executive, one of the main things he'd better do to help himself and to be effective in his work is to get along well with others. Not that an executive has to win popularity contests. He doesn't. Sometimes he is more respected than loved. Occasionally, he has few friendly relations with his associates and mainly comes into contact with them in cool, impersonal ways.

Nonetheless!—a first-rate leader would better be able to relate to his fellow workers pretty well. This means that it is desirable for him to be trusted by them; to have a considerable amount of support and loyalty from them;

to have them want to cooperate with him; to maintain friendly, though not necessarily intimate, relations with them. This also means that it is desirable for him to know how to bolster their egos; to refrain from cruelly criticizing them and putting them down; to avoid losing his temper with them; to treat them with fairness and kindness. This furthermore means that he is usually more effective if he doesn't act too conceitedly or egotistically when around his associates; that he is cooperative and helpful with them, especially when they get into vocational or personal difficulties; that he doesn't make empty promises to them; and that he has sufficiently good rapport with them so that, whenever he is in need of special help, they are quite willing to go beyond the call of duty to aid him. This finally means that, although he often has to be quite directive- and ultimatum-giving, he is not an arrant dictator or a smart-ass. His order-giving tone is, "Look, this would better be done for these reasons, and let's have no nonsense about it," rather than, "My will must absolutely be served, and you're part of the scum of the earth who are born and reared to serve me!"

All this, naturally, is much easier said than done. In order to get into and to maintain good relations with other people, whether you do so in the course of your business and organizational affairs or in your more personal life, you would better know what to do and have some talent at doing it. In addition, it is almost imperative that you not be significantly blocked by your own feelings of inadequacy and hostility. When you loathe yourself, you are likely to need people's approval desperately and to do all kinds of foolish things to win it; and not only will this not work with them, it may sabotage your relationship with others. For Jones, whose acceptance and love you think you direly need, sees that you will lick his boots to get it, and he usually loses a great deal of respect for you—and perhaps takes serious advantage of you. And Smith, who notes that you inordinately crave Jones's approval, also tends to lose respect for you. In addition, he may jealously hate you for not seeming to need him as much as you need Jones. Lots of internecine corporate wars, some of them involving a great many people in the same organization, start from this type of reverberating love need. Then, to make matters worse, other love slobs in your outfit—such as Roe, who thinks that he requires everyone's liking—upset themselves because you are hung up on Jones; Smith is pissed off at (and hence inordinately preoccupied with) you; and various other people are so engrossed in your, Jones's, and Smith's doings, that they feel almost totally neglected, and they become disturbed and ineffectual. More negative reverberations!

Hostility, naturally, is even worse. You, because of your hang-ups, become hostile toward Cohen; and he usually makes himself equally hostile to you. Your boss (who is also Cohen's) sees the two of you sabotaging each other's activity. So he becomes mad at both of you. The president of your firm sees all kinds of enmities occurring; and he becomes generally angry himself at the negative conditions that ensue. Before you know it, almost everyone, not to mention everyone's wife, is hating everybody else, and near-chaos reigns.

Let's take a more specific look at some of the emotional upsets that may easily interfere with your people relations, to see what you can do about uncreating them. At point A, the Activating Event, you find that one of the other executives in your organization, who has been employed there just about the same amount of time as you have and has equivalent age, education, and previous experience to yours, is doing remarkably well in handling his department. The higher officers of the firm are beginning spontaneously to make favorable comments about him, while they rarely seem to be doing the same about you. At point C, you began to feel terribly inadequate about this, to avoid this other executive (with whom you previously may have had very friendly relations), to feel uncomfortable when you're around the company officers, and to become more and more critical of many of the people under you. Before you know it, your personal relations with your co-workers are seriously impaired and you begin wondering whether you can really get along with anybody. You read some good books on how to win friends and influence people, and they help a little. But, frankly, you don't *feel like* being very friendly, and you often feel like telling half the world to go fuck itself. In fact, on some days you do.

At point B, you first have a rational Belief about your fellow executive's doing remarkably well and your not equaling his achievements: "Damn! I wish to hell he weren't so capable—or maybe lucky. Or, more honestly, I wish *I* were doing as well as he. And it is really deplorable that I'm not. At this rate, he's going to get that higher managerial job I wanted; he's going to make considerably more money than I; and if I don't watch it, the comparisons between our work may lead to my demotion or my being fired. What a pain in the ass!"

If you stayed rigorously with these rational Beliefs, you wouldn't feel ecstatically happy, but you wouldn't feel miserable either. You would mainly feel disappointed and frustrated; and these feelings might help you by motivating you to work harder, to curry more favor with your superiors, to treat the people under you better, and otherwise to take some sensible steps to catch up with or compensate for the phenomenal success of your associate. That would be fine; and his success might even be helpful to you. Or, at the very least, it might encourage you to cement some of your personal relationships with other members of the firm.

But quite irrationally, instead, you tend to lap over to a different, and essentially magical Belief: "How could he behave like that—showing everyone that he is doing far better than I am, and getting me into such trouble? I hate his goddamned guts! What a terrible thing to happen to me! This proves what an idiot and an incompetent I am! And then I foolishly make myself so upset about this, too. *That's* great behavior, isn't it? I'm such a nincompoop that I'll never be able to get myself out of this mess!"

What can you do about these self-defeating, insane Beliefs? As usual, Dispute them—at point D—until you see how untenable they are and until you start consistently giving them up. Thus, you could challenge yourself (and give much saner answers to your challenges) as follows:

Question: "Why can't he behave exactly as he is be-having, even though I may get into trouble if he keeps outdoing my performances?" Answer: "Of course he can! He has a perfect right to do whatever he does. That is his nature, to act like *he* acts and not like *I* would want him to act. It is unfortunate if I get into trouble because he is excelling me in many ways. So it's unfortunate! But that's the way conditions around me often are—unfortu-nate. Now, what am I going to do to try to make them a little *less* unfortunate? There's no point in my hating his guts, in spite of his causing me a good deal of trouble. Even if he acts badly, I would better only hate his *acts* and not *him*. But he hasn't acted badly toward me. He has merely done what he wants to do and is capable of doing; and I am only artificially relating his acts to me."

Question: "Why is this thing that has happened to me so terrible?" Answer: "It is certainly damned inconven-ient! At least, I think it is—though in the final analysis, it may even prove to be convenient. If he, by his behavior, shows that things can be done better in our organization, then I may learn by his behavior and do better myself. Maybe he's even helped me in this regard. But even if he has not, and even if I never do any better and he merely excels me, it's *only* disadvantageous; it's never *awful*. If the worst comes to the worst, and I get demoted or fired because of his actions, it's still not awful. It's just one of the harsh facts of life. And there's no reason why I can't be a pretty happy human being, in spite of these harsh facts."

Question: "Where is the evidence that I am an idiot and an incompetent, just because he may be brighter and more competent than I?" Answer: "There isn't any, of course. Practically no human being is *an* idiot or *an* incompetent. Even those who are institutionalized for mental deficiency generally do *some* things well; and to call *them* idiots (instead of individuals who often perform idiotically) is to make a silly overgeneralization. As for me, I do lots of things intelligently and well. So I am probably a person who usually behaves astutely and ably, but who sometimes does not and who often does not do *as* well as someone else does. How interesting that, in this respect, I am typically human!"

Question: "How does it prove, just because I foolishly upset myself about this situation, that I am such a blasted nincompoop that I'll never be able to get myself out of this mess?" Answer: "It doesn't! Naturally, if I continue to upset myself this way, I shall have more difficulty extricating myself from this mess than if I don't upset myself. Therefore, I'd be wiser if I didn't. But even if I continue to upset myself like this, I shall only make things more difficult and not necessarily impossible. Other easily upsettable people extricate themselves from messes. Why shouldn't I be able to do so?"

If you persist, along these or similar lines, in Disputing your irrational Beliefs which produce your woeful feelings of inadequacy and the inertia and inefficiency that tend to accompany them, the chances are that you will mobilize your actions more effectively and do something to help yourself overcome your associate's competition. You may or may not compete better with him, in the process, but you will at least *feel better* about your being less highly thought of than he.

The next way that you tend to make things worse for yourself in this kind of situation is to dwell on making yourself feel exceptionally angry and rebellious. Thus, in the same situation that we are hypothesizing at point A —one of the other executives in your firm doing much better than you and winning favor from you with the higher officers of your organization—you can experience, at point C, keen resentment in addition to or instead of self-deprecation. For after rationally telling yourself, at point B, that you don't like this executive's or the higher-ups' behavior, you can feed yourself these extremely irrational Beliefs:

"What a worm he is for showing off to the officers as he is doing! He probably isn't even doing half so well as he seems to be. He's merely convincing them, cleverly and falsely, that he is. What gall! As for them, they're stupidly seeing the best in him, when it may not even be that good; and then they're nastily ignoring my good work, expecting me to perform utter miracles, and not giving me half the credit I deserve for all I've done for the firm these past years. What ingratitude! What injustice! How can everyone be like that—so neglectful and nasty to me—when I try so hard and really have the best interests of the company at heart?"

These irrational Beliefs of yours are complete nonsense. Although they may have some factual data behind them, they jump to unwarranted conclusions that have nothing at all to do with these data. They take one of the common grim facts of life and weave it into a web of abysmal horror. Why? Because:

1. Suppose the executive who is doing such a "good"

job and is helping make you look like something of a clod really isn't doing as well as he seems to be doing on the surface, is cleverly snowing your superior officers, and is behaving falsely. Well, why shouldn't he? Wouldn't you do the same, if you could get away with it? And even if you wouldn't, does that mean he shouldn't? It would be lovely—at least for you—if he were as honest and sincere as you are. But he isn't! And why must he be what he isn't? Why can't you realistically make allowances for his actual behavior—instead of *demanding* that it be different—and make some kind of effective adjustment to it? Perhaps, even, sagely copy it!

2. Why do you see this competing executive as being full of gall for doing what he's doing? Certainly, he seems to be self-assertive. But does he really have impudence and effrontery, merely because he's doing what you are not? Besides, suppose he *does* have gall. Why should he not have it? Because you don't have it? Because most people may not have it? Who said he ought to be exactly like you or like most people? Why can't he choose his own gall-filled way, if that's what he wants to do?

3. Just because the people in the upper echelon in your organization are permitting themselves to be impressed by your rival, how does this prove that they are nastily ignoring your good work, expecting you to perform miracles, and not giving you half the credit you deserve? Maybe all these hypotheses of yours are true; but maybe they are merely ego-bolstering rationalizations on your part. Where is the *evidence* you can muster to confirm these assumptions? Besides, let's suppose that all these hypotheses are valid and that your superiors are

truly prejudiced against you and are not giving you the
credit you deserve. So? Isn't that their prerogative—to
make mistakes of this sort? Aren't they entitled to their
prejudices against you? *Must* they be biased in your
favor, or at least neutral? Why must they?

4. Are the higher-ups in your firm really as ungrateful
and unjust to you as you think they are? How can you
prove this assertion? And if they are filled with ingratitude and injustice, is that so uncommon among human
beings? Are you the only one in the world, or even in
your company, who was ever so unfairly treated? Not
likely! This does not mean, of course, that ingratitude
and injustice are good. They are bad. But why shouldn't
bad things exist in the universe and in your life? You act
as if the world is so ordered that anything of a truly inequitable nature cannot possibly exist in it—especially
when it is inequitable to *you*. But of course it can! People
have no difficulty whatever in being ungrateful and unfair. Why should your superiors be the exception to this
pretty general rule? Because you would *like* them to be
an exception? Fine: go on liking. But you'd better stop
demanding that you get what you like!

Thus, with arguments such as these, you could go on
to point D and Dispute your irrational Beliefs about the
obnoxious Activating Events at point A. If you did such
Disputing, you would probably come up with two new
philosophies or cognitive Effects, at point E:

One: "It is really a nuisance when someone with
whom I work does much better than I do and wins much
more acclaim from our superiors. But that's the way it
goes. There's often someone who will better me in vari-

ous kinds of performances, and I certainly have little or no control over the way he behaves. Now, why don't I focus on other people and things? Thus I may realize that his work actually says nothing about mine, and see that, even if I never do as well as he or win as much favor with the higher-ups in our firm, it won't mean that I can't improve in the future or that I *should* do much better and am a total nincompoop when I don't do what I *should*. There are no *shoulds* in the universe!—only a hell of a lot of *it would be betters!*"

Two: "There's no good reason why, even when I'm doing my best, others have to appreciate my efforts and treat me fairly. I shall naturally try to arrange this kind of treatment, and may even choose, when feasible, to work with those people who generally give it. But that's only an ideal, and one that I often may not be able to achieve. When I am unjustly or ungratefully assessed, it's highly undesirable. But that's *all* it is: undesirable, disadvantageous, handicapping. And I can still be happy, and often get along very well, in an undesirable, disadvantageous, and handicapping situation. Not that I don't *want* justice. I do. But why the devil do I *need* it? Clearly, I don't."

If you arrive at these two basic attitudes, and truly believe in them most of the time, you may still have feelings of inadequacy and hostility that will sometimes interfere with your relationships with others. But not significantly or often. You will then be running your own life rather than letting external situations, at A, and your disordered feelings, at C, run you.

7 Achieving self-discipline

It almost goes without saying that an effective executive would better be quite self-disciplined. For if he is not able to train himself to give up present pleasures for future gains, and thereby to set a reasonably good example for those who work under him, it is not likely that he will gain their admiration or respect or encourage them to control their own behavior for their and for the organization's good.

The executive's very functioning, moreover, often depends on the strictness with which he is able to abide by certain sensible rules of living. By and large, the busy organizational leader requires a considerable amount of good health and high energy; and it is unlikely that he is going to achieve these goals if he is careless and sloppy about hygienic regimen. If he is wise, for example, the aspirant to leadership will eat regularly and well (and, especially, refrain from overeating); will get a sufficient amount of sleep most nights; will go easy on such enjoyments as drinking and smoking; will get regular medical checkups and follow his physician's prescriptions; will exercise adequately; and will stick to various other sane rules of health. This is not to say that he will be an angel in these respects; but at least he will not be a habitual goofer.

Assuming that he is sufficiently self-disciplined to abide by a reasonable set of hygienic rules, the efficient executive would better also exert a high degree of self-control in his work and life involvements. For even the most fascinating and exciting jobs contain, inevitably, a lot of routine and boring activities; and intelligent and creative people particularly find such activities a bore. But if they tend to avoid them, their other work falls apart, they antagonize many of the people with whom they work, and they frequently fall so far behind in appointments, deadlines, and other job requirements that either chaos ensues or they barely get by instead of performing up to their best potentials.

As an executive, therefore, you'd better learn to accept drudgery when it is a necessary part of your work; to persist at many tasks even when you are no longer interested in them; to do often what is most important rather than what you would rather do at the moment; to put up with lots of people whom, in your personal life, you would hardly stomach for a few minutes; to meet important deadlines even when they are arbitrarily and foolishly set; to keep your mouth shut on many occasions when you are bitterly thinking that Mr. So-and-So is a nitwit or that Miss Such-and-Such would do the company a favor by dropping dead.

The problem is not *what* to discipline yourself about. That is usually obvious—indeed, painfully so. The problem is, *how*. Dr. Robert A. Harper and I gave the answer to this question a number of years ago in our book *A Guide to Rational Living* (Englewood Cliffs, N.J.: Prentice-Hall, 1961; paperback edition, Hollywood: Wilshire Books, 1971). We pointed out that lack of discipline is usually caused by a basic irrational idea, which literally millions of individuals believe: The idea that it is easier to avoid facing many life difficulties and self-responsibilities than to undertake more rewarding forms of self-discipline. This idea can be actively and vigorously combated in a number of ways, which we listed in the book:

"1. Although the taking on of needless tasks and responsibilities is not to be highly recommended, and is often a manifestation of masochism, you'd better determine what are the truly necessary activities of life—and then unrebellingly and promptly perform them. Necessary life tasks usually include: (a) tasks which are strictly necessary for existence, such as eating, defecating, building a shelter from the cold, and so forth; and (b) tasks which are not strictly necessary for survival but that must be performed if one wishes to obtain desired goals. For example, brushing one's teeth to ensure their not decaying, or commuting in order to live in the country and work in the city.

"2. Once you decide that a goal is necessary for your survival or highly desirable for your happiness (and not because *others* think you should attain it), self-discipline in regard to this goal can be attained by vigorous self-propagandization and forced action. In particular, you'd better first ferret out and forcefully attack your main *un*-disciplining internal verbalizations: the nonsense you keep telling yourself along the lines of 'It is easier for me to remain the way I am,' 'I don't believe that I *can* discipline myself,' and 'Why should I *have* to do these unpleasant things in order to get the pleasant results I desire?' Instead, work to acquire a philosophy of life represented by these kinds of sentences: 'It is definitely harder and less rewarding, especially in the long run, for me to do things the "easy way" '; 'I *do* have the ability, as a human being, to discipline myself, even though it is quite difficult to do so'; and 'Whether I like it or not, there *is* no other way to get the pleasant results I desire than by doing the unpleasant and time-consuming requisites to these results.'

"3. You'd better face the fact that, because you are a fallible human being, you often will have great difficulty getting started along a certain constructive line, and that normal principles of inertia will tend to hold you back and make the starting process quite a chore. *Expect,* therefore, these problems to occur and prophylactically *accept* the fact that you will often have to use *extra* push and *extra* energy to get yourself on the road to self-discipline. Once you get going at brushing your teeth or getting up in the morning to travel to work, your task will tend to get easier and sometimes, even, enjoyable. But at the start it is *not* usually easy; and you'd better not expect it to be. Easy or not, keep convincing yourself that, if you want to obtain certain present or future results, there simply *is* no other way and it is to your advantage (or sometimes your lesser disadvantage) to discipline yourself in a given manner.

"4. Once you start on any self-disciplining task, you can sometimes make things easier for yourself: put yourself on some kind of a regular schedule or program; give yourself some subgoals on any major project that you undertake; work on a piece rate basis (for example, force yourself to write so many pages or do a certain minimum number of exercises a day); or give yourself some intermediate rewards for your disciplining (permit yourself to go to a movie *after* you have completed this much studying or that much house cleaning for the day).

"5. Guard against leaning over backward to be *too* self-disciplined or to do things the *too* hard way in order to achieve some magical rewards for your self-punishment. Most kinds of rigid adherence to rules, on the one hand, or inflexible rebelliousness against them, on the other hand, tend to be a throwing out of the baby with the bath water and stem from emotional disturbance. Overdisciplining yourself can be just as self-defeating as avoidance of necessary discipline.

"In sum: it *is* very difficult for the average or even the

above-average individual to keep fighting against his or her normal tendencies to give up easily on hard tasks, to put off till tomorrow what really is best done today, and to slacken self-discipline long before it automatically develops its own momentum and begins to maintain itself with relatively little effort. All right, so it's hard. But it still continually has to be done if innumerable life responsibilities are to be adequately faced and solved and if long-range hedonism is to be appreciably achieved. And there *is* no other way. Avoid or cavil as you may, the piper still is to be paid. If *your* goals and desires are to be attained, *you* would better accept—and we really mean *accept*—steady self-discipline. Tough. But that's what being human essentially means."

Disciplining yourself, if you are an executive, does not significantly differ from self-regulation if you work in almost any other kind of capacity. It mainly entails the acceptance of the fact that there are several important time limitations in the life of practically everyone. And that includes you. You will probably only live for about seventy-five years. You will spend a good deal of those years sleeping, traveling to and from work, and doing many uncreative chores. Whether you like it or not, you will have to occupy many hours, some of them almost entirely wasted, with your associates. And you will be lucky, all told, to have left even a reasonably extended period each day and each week to do and to supervise the kind of work you would like to see done. Since time is of the essence—since it is the one aspect of existence which you can least stretch—what are you going to do with it? The sensible answer is: Discipline yourself so that you can best use the amount of it which is truly available.

Fine! But your resolve to regulate your ways intelligently and efficiently is merely a pious hope unless you are emotionally free to do so. And freedom in this respect includes (as perhaps almost all personal freedom includes) emancipation from short-range hedonism and from the dire need for others' approval. For if you are addicted to these values, your chances of being highly self-disciplined are about as good as your chances of painting a great portrait when you are blindfolded.

Let us now consider some of the main emotional blocks to self-discipline and see what you can specifically do to unfetter yourself in this regard. Suppose, first, you have, at point A, a fairly demanding wife and a couple of children; your mother and father are hardly in the best health, and keeping asking for attention; you are still completing some educational requirements that will help you in your main field of endeavor; and you are doing well enough in your executive position, but you also have many hassles in getting important things done and reaching the kind of higher position that you want to reach. In sum, you are a somewhat typical executive in a somewhat typical position in life and in work! Consequently, you know perfectly well that in order to achieve your chosen ends, you'd better be quite disciplined in a number of ways.

But—at point C—you definitely are not. Your health regimens are far from ideal; you are spending too much time on extended, pleasurable lunch hours during the day and on poker games (or something similar) into the wee hours at night; and when important conferences or interviews are scheduled, you tend to show up late or to put them off entirely at the last minute.

Well, what are you saying to yourself, at point B, to cause this undisciplined behavior at point C? For one thing, you are snowing yourself with short-range hedonistic philosophies. Thus, you are first sanely telling yourself, at your rational Belief: "Damn! It's really hard keeping myself in line! I just don't have enough time to get to the gym for at least half an hour a day; to devote myself to my wife and kids for the hour or two that would keep them happy; to get in the recreation that makes me much better able to face each busy day; and to do as much work as I'd truly like to do. If each day were just one and a half times as long, it would barely be enough! How stupidly limiting life is for an energetic, hell-bent-for-joy-*and*-achievement guy like me! It's just not fair."

If you strictly stayed with this rational Belief, at B, you would have a somewhat unpleasant emotional Consequence, at C; and we would call that Consequence feelings of frustration, annoyance, and irritation, and you would live not too badly with them.

But we know that you feel *more* than that, at C; and that an essentially bright fellow, like you, is idiotically screwing himself, at C, with goofing behavior that is making him not only overrebellious but also actively self-sabotaging. Therefore, we'd better look for the highly *irrational* Belief that you also hold at B. And this irrational Belief—or set of Beliefs—seems to be something along these lines: "It's *horribly* hard for me to keep myself disciplined. I shouldn't *have* to keep to these *awful* time limitations. I simply *must* have more time each day than is actually available! Considering how hard-working and talented I am, life just ought not to *be* that unfair!"

It is this utter hogwash, this asinine refusal on your part to stay within the bounds of reality, that is destroying you and nuttily *creating* the Consequences (or neurotic symptoms) that you are experiencing at point C. Now, how would you go about Disputing, at point C, your own hogwash?

As follows. You would ask yourself:

"Why is it *horribly* hard for me to keep myself in line?" And you would (sooner or later) reply: "It isn't! Indeed, if there is anything *horribly* difficult, it is to keep myself *out* of line. For the line of least resistance, the line of keeping myself *away* from the gym, *from* enjoying my wife and children, and *at* playing poker until 3 A.M. once or twice a week, honestly amounts to the line of *most* resistance from my own life choices. Nobody but me *wants* to keep in good physical health, *wants* to enjoy my wife and children, and *wants* to attend to my executive tasks in a bright and chipper way. If I *don't* desire these things, then I'd better consciously make other choices: give up my gym subscription, divorce my family, and get a nice, comfy civil service berth or something like that. But if I really *choose* physical fitness, family life, and executive alertness I can't simultaneously choose absence from gym, family neglect, and playing poker until 3 A.M. It's too bad I can't have all these things at once; but I can't!"

Question: "Who says I shouldn't *have* to keep to these *awful* time limitations?" Response: "No one says so, except—quite foolishly!—me. Theoretically, I don't *have* to do anything: I don't have to live, to hold a job, to be efficient, or anything else like that. But once I *choose* to live, there are *then* things I have to do to implement this choice: such as eat and drink. And once I *choose* to be healthy, have a wife and family, and be a competent executive, then I pretty well have to keep to time limitations that almost automatically go with these choices. Calling such time limitations *awful*, moreover, is ridiculous. They are often onerous and restricting. I'll probably never greatly enjoy them. But *awful* means they *should* not exist because they are onerous and restricting; and who the hell am I to say they *should* not? Once I rule the entire universe, I'll probably arrange things so that frustrating time limitations never exist—at least not for *me!* But until that time, I'd better accept the fact that they do!"

Question: "Why *must* I have more time each day than is actually available?" Reply: "Because I, of course, am God. Because the ordinary rules of the universe just don't hold for a Noble Person like me. Because, marvel that I am, I *deserve* special consideration from the world that lesser lights than I don't deserve. What crap! No matter how talented I may be, I am still not a Special Person—merely a person who may have some special traits. And, no matter how many such traits I may have, I still live in the regular universe and am subject to its laws and vicissitudes. The sun and the earth did not stand still for the Beethovens, Leonardos, or Dostoevskis. Why should they change their courses for me?"

Question: "Is it true that, considering how hard-working and talented I am, life just ought not *be* that unfair?" Answer: "Like hell it is! Why is it unfair, anyway, if I only have about seventy-five years to live and twenty-four hours a day in which to live them? As long as it was fair for me to be born, why is it unjust and unethical for me to be limited by the human condition into which I was born? And even suppose it *is* unfair for me to be time-limited (because I would be happier if I were not), who said that unfairness shouldn't exist? Jehovah? Jesus? Pollyanna? A hell of a lot they knew! It *does* exist. It *is,* during my lifetime at least, here to stay. Tough titty! Now how can I at least be fair to myself and tolerate, if never enjoy, the inevitable inequities of human existence?"

Rational Sensitivity shows you how, with the logico-empirical method of questioning and challenging, to Dispute (at point D) your irrational Beliefs (at point B), so that you finally come up with (at point E) a new cognitive or philosophic Effect. And that is? That it is hard to accept time limits and discipline yourself by giving up present pleasures for future gains. But it is not *too* hard if you really want the gains and if you choose to go after them instead of the present pleasures. Discipline almost always requires some amount of sacrifice. If you aren't willing to make such sacrifices, then you don't have to whine about the advantages you will lose from lack of discipline.

What about dire love need? How does that interfere with sensible self-regulation? In a number of important ways, such as the one we shall now use for illustrative purposes.

You have, at point A again, the same demanding wife and children, sick parents, educational requirements you are completing, and hassles at your executive position. And, at point C, you are behaving in an undisciplined manner about keeping up with these demands—not because you are a short-range hedonist but because you are a love slob. For, instead of doing what you have chosen to do, you spend inordinate amounts of time with some of your friends and other people in your industry, boozing it up, talking about their problems, playing golf, and otherwise maintaining good relationships with them.

At point B, your Belief System, you are first rationally convincing yourself: "Isn't it too bad that I don't have as much time as I would prefer to have for my friends and acquaintances? But I just don't. I would like very much to have more of their approval, and it's sad that I don't have the time to devote to getting it. How annoying!" If you stayed with this rational (albeit negative) Belief, you would merely feel disappointed and frustrated; but hardly very upset.

Being human, however, you tend to lap over into a distinctly irrational set of Beliefs: "Isn't it *terrible* that I don't have as much time as I would like to have for my friends and acquaintances! I must *make* such time, no matter what! I absolutely *need* more approval from them, and it's *awful* that I don't have more time to devote to getting it. I can't tolerate this state of affairs; so I've *got* to say Yes to my friends when they ask me out, even though I know I can't afford the time." These irrational Beliefs encourage—hell, practically *force*—you to spend inordinate amounts of time with your friends and to shirk many of the important things you'd better do to succeed as an executive.

Rational Sensitivity helps you to challenge love-slobbism in several ways. First, it sensitizes you to the fact that A doesn't lead to C, and that the mere fact that you have so many real demands on you doesn't *make* you undisciplined. Secondly, it shows you how to look for B —your rational and irrational Beliefs that really lead to the Consequences that you are experiencing at C. Thirdly, it contends that irrational Beliefs are only hypotheses, constructs, and assumptions—rather than facts or data—and that they can always be challenged and changed. Fourthly, it provides you with a logical and an empirical method of Disputing these hypotheses—at point D—until you finally decide that they are not valid and consequently surrender them.

More specifically, Rational Sensitivity enables you to do this kind of Disputing of your love-slob abetting assumptions:

Question: "Why is it *terrible* that I don't have as much time as I would like to have for my friends and acquaintances?" Rejoinder: "It's no more terrible to have little time for this pursuit than it is to have relatively little time for playing the piano or reading Shakespeare. The only thing I can lose in life is pleasure; and in order to get pleasure Number 1 I often have to give up some of pleasure Numbers 2, 3, and 4. If I don't see my friends as often as I would like to see them, that will make me deprived; but that's *all* it will make me. O.K., so I'll then be deprived. But I'd much rather be deprived of some of their companionship, than of having close relations with my wife and children, contributing some joy to my mother and father before they die, completing this course which will help me considerably with my work, and attending to my job performances and improving myself considerably as an executive. Since life has to have some important deprivations, why is *this* one so terrible? Obviously, it isn't!"

Question: "Where is the evidence that I *need* more approval from my friends and acquaintances and that it's *awful* that I don't have more time to devote to getting this?" Answer: "Need, schmeed! *Need* is really a short word for *necessity*. Now, is it really *necessary* that I get more approval from my friends and acquaintances? Will I die without it? Acquire cancer? Become a Bowery bum? Shit, no! I don't even *need* to become an effective executive. But I damned well *want* to do so; and if that is what I really want, I'd better not let these made-up 'needs' interfere with that want. It would be nice and convenient if I had so much time available that I could devote it to (1) being an outstanding executive *and* (2) getting more approval from my friends. But it's hardly *awful* if that niceness and convenience doesn't exist."

Question: "In what way can't I tolerate this state of affairs?" Reply: "I'll probably never be deliriously happy about it. I wish to hell it would change. But why can't I *tolerate* what I don't like? Because, obviously, I think I'm a baby who *must* get exactly what he wants, and immediately; and it is that crazy *belief* of mine which makes me so intolerant of any frustration. Well, *am* I a baby—or do I just *think* I am? Clearly, I'm not. But if I continue to think I am, and act as if I am, I shall be pretty indistinguishable from a baby, no matter what my chronological age happens to be!"

If you continue to Dispute your irrational Beliefs that create your love-slobbism, and hence interfere with your self-discipline, you will finally tend to end up, at E, with a cognitive Effect of this sort: "Yes, it would be nice if my friends and acquaintances approved of me and if I were able to spend more time with them and abet this kind of approval; but nice doesn't mean necessary. I can lead a very good life, with or without their full approval. And there are other goals, such as efficient executive functioning, which are in some ways even more enjoyable than having others approve of me, and that are certainly less dependent on the ups and downs of their lives. So why don't I choose to spend *some* time with my friends and win *some* approbation from them, and also spend considerable time following my other life goals and disciplining myself so I can follow them adequately?"

If, I hypothesize, you achieve and maintain this kind of philosophy, you will overcome most of your shirking tendencies and be able to discipline yourself in a suitable manner. What is more, you will tend to give up the inclination toward overausterity or exaggerated discipline for the sake of discipline. For that, too, is usually the result of a kind of love-slobbism. Thus, at point A, you have good reasons for regulating and planning your life, and for giving up some present enjoyments for future rewards, but at C you behave in a highly ascetic, automatonlike, joyless manner. You allow yourself virtually *no* golf or card-playing; you *never* see your friends; you *only* get to work early in the morning and leave late at night. You resort to these extremes, moreover, not because you truly like this kind of a life, but because (at point B), you irrationally Believe: "I *must* be completely self-disciplined. No one will respect me at all if I allow myself the slightest bit of shirking. What a worm I would be if I was in the slightest way self-indulgent and was not a 110 percent machinelike executive!"

This kind of thinking is closely related to love-slobbism because it essentially demands that you be utterly self-controlled—not for practical purposes or to insure later enjoyments in life—but so that others will love and respect you and so that you will ultimately get into some kind of heaven for such noble behavior. You are therefore not disciplining yourself for *you* but for *what others (including the angels) think of you;* and that is the essence of love-slobbism.

Rational Sensitivity, therefore, shows you that both under- and overdiscipline can be emotionally unhealthful and can interfere with executive (and personal) efficiency. The fundamental goal of life, if you are truly sane, is to increase your short-range and long-range enjoyments, and is not to achieve for the sake of achieving or for the sake of having others deify you. To be rationally sensitized to yourself means to discover what *you* really want out of the one existence you are likely ever to

have. What others may want you to want may be interesting and (if in some way this knowledge is used for
your own ends) even valuable. But the primary question
of life still is: What do *you* really want, for now and for
the future? Self-discipline (and other goals that you
choose) would better be seen in the framework of that
kind of question.

8 Creating self-acceptance

The most valuable of all human traits, for the executive as well as for almost every other human being, is probably full self-acceptance. And not only does the average organization person not have this, he really does not know what it is.

This is hardly strange, since few *psychologists* appear to know what self-acceptance is. They continually confuse and confound it with "self-confidence," "self-esteem," "self-approval," "self-love," and other traits of that ilk which in many respects are not only different from true self-acceptance but are antithetical to it.

Unconditional self-acceptance means exactly what it seems to mean: that the individual fully accepts *himself,* his existence, his being, his aliveness, without any requirements or conditions whatsoever. On the other hand, what we usually call "self-confidence" or "self-esteem" is highly *conditional* acceptance of the individual by himself. For if you have confidence in yourself or esteem yourself, you almost invariably do it for some *reason:* because you do something *well*. And if this is so, you lose that confidence or that esteem just as soon as you consistently begin to function poorly in that same area.

I tried to make this distinction clear some years ago in my book, *Reason and Emotion in Psychotherapy* (New York: Lyle Stuart, Inc., 1962). I distinguished there among (1) work-confidence (or achievement-confidence), (2) love-confidence, and (3) self-confidence. Work-confidence essentially means that you are telling yourself, "I have done this task before and succeeded at it several times, and therefore I am confident that I can do it successfully again." Love-confidence means that you are convincing yourself something like, "I have been able to win this person's (or these people's) approval before, and I am pretty sure that I can do it again." Neither work-confidence nor love-confidence, however, provide true *self*-confidence, or a sense of personal worth, since they imply, "If I lose the ability to work well or if I no longer am able to win people's approval, then I am a pretty worthless individual. For only *by* achieving and *by* winning love do I make myself worthwhile." Self-confidence, on the other hand, implies, "I am determined *always* to accept myself *whether or not* I succeed at various tasks and *whether or not* I win people's approval."

Self-confidence, in other words, is *not* related to external props, to achieving success or winning approval, but is gained by *definition*. I fully accept myself merely because I *decide* to fully accept myself; and I do not need any special *reason* to do so. Since writing *Reason and Emotion in Psychotherapy*, I have dropped the term *self-confidence* (along with terms such as *self-esteem, self-love*, and *self-approval*) and I have also dropped the term "unconditional positive regard" (which was coined by the famous psychotherapist, Carl Rogers), because they all imply that the individual must *rate* or *measure* himself in some manner; and the only way he could really do so would be in accordance with some performance. Thus, if I have high self-esteem or high regard for myself, I must have done *something* to deserve it; and if I fail to do that something well in the future, I will end up with low self-esteem or low regard for myself. Moreover, even when I have high self-esteem, since I can always do poorly in the future, I remain underlyingly anxious about losing my self-esteem. So I never quite solve the problem of consistently and fully accepting myself, and I always remain in real danger of hating myself.

I therefore now use the term *self-acceptance* (or *self-choosing*) because I think it is a more neutral word, and doesn't imply *any* rating of the self. I am opposed, in fact, to all self-judgment, for it cannot be philosophically justified, and it leads to poor results in almost all cases. For my *self* or my *being* that I am rating is infinitely complex, is an ongoing process, and consists of hundreds (perhaps thousands) of traits and performances. It is virtually impossible to give it, at any one time, a single global rating and by this rating to say that *I* am "good," "bad," or "indifferent." My tennis game, or psychotherapeutic ability, or appearance, or almost any other trait may be justifiably rated or assessed; but even if I knew what the ratings of all these traits accurately were (and would be in the future), how could I possibly get a single rating of *me, myself, my being?*

Self-ratings, moreover, invariably imply deification and devilifying. For the real reason I want to say, "*I* am good because I have done this and that good thing," is that I am trying to prove that I am better than *you,* and in fact better than *everyone,* and in fact worthy of getting to heaven and sitting on the right hand side of God. And the real reason, if I am honest about it, that I want to say, "*I* am bad because I have these and those bad traits," is that I am trying to prove that I am worse than you, and in fact worse than everyone else, and in fact worthy of being condemned to hell and being the henchman of the devil.

The nonelegant solution to the proglem of ego, worth, or feelings of adequacy is the one that Robert Harper and I gave in *A Guide to Rational Living.* Using this solution, you rate your *traits* and *performances* but not your *self;* and if you consider yourself to have worth at all, you say, "I am good not because I do well or am loved by others, but merely because I am alive. My goodness is my aliveness. Period." This is a highly practical solution to the problem of human worth, in that it sets up a simple standard for your value that is not dependent on anything you do or on any opinion of you that others may have. Since you will only have value or worth while you live, and since you will not ask yourself at all, once you are dead, what your worth is, you will always, by this standard, be "good," "valuable," or "worthy" as an individual just as long as you are still living. What could be a safer standard than that?

In my more recent writings and teachings, however, I have given a more elegant solution. For, philosophically, it is untenable to say, "I am good because I am alive," or "I am a worthy person because I exist," because this is a tautological or definitional statement and can never be proven or disproven. You could just as "validly" say, "I am bad because I am alive," and that would be definitional, and unprovable or disprovable, too. Consequently, the more elegant solution is never to rate yourself in *any* way, but only to rate your traits, characteristics, deeds, and performances.

Thus, you could justifiably say: "(1) I am alive. (2) I choose to continue to live. (3) I desire, while I am living, to have relatively little pain and much pleasure. (4) Now, let me see how I can manage to decrease my pain and increase my short-range and long-range pleasure." With this philosophic attitude, you could then rate your traits as much as you wanted to—note, for example, that you were good at arithmetic and hockey and poor at spelling and tennis—in order to improve the poor ones (when feasible and possible) and to live peacefully with the bad ones (for example, avoid becoming a secretary if you are poor at spelling). And you would never have to rate your self, your being, your existence at all. Or, another way of putting it: You could always accept yourself, your aliveness, your existence, and determine to have as much joy out of life as you could possibly have during this existence, no matter how you rated your traits. You would naturally *prefer* to have certain high-rated or "good" abilities (such as the ability to read well or be a good sportsman) because such characteristics would often bring you increased pleasure. But you would not *need* to have these "good" abilities in order to feel worthwhile or to accept your self.

This kind of full acceptance of your existence, and firm determination to enjoy it as much as possible in the here and now as well as in the future, I call *self-acceptance* (or *self-choosing*). This is a more neutral term than *self-esteem* or *self-love* because it does not imply the ego-rating that such terms do. And although to "like yourself," to have "great ego-strength," or to "think a great deal of yourself" seem, on the surface, to be fine characteristics for you to have, they are really quite dangerous. For if you have a "good ego," this really means that you are rating yourself—not merely your traits and performances, but your *self*—very highly; and that it may well only be a matter of time before you have a "poor ego," or rate yourself poorly. Whenever you invent mythical ego heavens, you almost inevitably invent mythical ego hells. It would be far better, if you merely accepted yourself, or did not rate *you,* your *being,* your *existence* at all.

Even the phrase "accept yourself" or "self-acceptance" has its distinct limitations and is inaccurate. For the individual's "self" or "ego" can hardly be defined, and is not too dissimilar from his "soul"—which is mainly a theological term without any empirical referent. If you want to be elegantly accurate, therefore, you will neither accept nor condemn yourself. Instead, you will accept the fact that you exist and that you have various traits; you will accept your existence with these traits, even when the latter are poor or undesirable; and you will accept the "goodness" or "badness"—or, more objectively, the inefficiency or efficiency—of these traits in regard to the likelihood of their helping you enjoy more pleasure and feel less pain.

Moreover, when you engage in this kind of "self-acceptance"—or, better, *you-acceptance*—you will have little difficulty in acknowledging the undesirability of many of your traits and in trying to change them while still accepting you. For your traits, while acceptable in the sense that they truly exist and would better not be denied, may definitely not be acceptable to you as desirable traits; and you may therefore want to find them "nonacceptable" or worth changing. You may consequently fully accept yourself (or the fact that you are alive and would better have a ball in life) while at the same time not accepting some of your behavior (the fact that you act in certain deplorable ways). And you may work very hard at continuing to accept *you* (even though this behavior still is deplorable) while changing those *aspects* of you (this deplorable behavior) which you would rather not put up with.

This is particularly true and important in regard to your being an efficient executive and a happy human being. For as an executive, there is invariably a large amount of your behavior that you do *not* want to accept —such as your inertia, incompetence, lack of discipline,

inability to get along with others, and self-deprecation.
Consequently, you'd better work hard at minimizing or
eliminating some of these traits. But you are unlikely to
do this if you keep berating yourself for having them. For
if you are a shit for doing a wrong, self-defeating act,
how can a shit like you do a correct, undefeating act in
the future? Anyone who (by definition) is a worm for
acting wormily will, because of his supposed wormhood,
tend to act consistently wormily in the future.

Only, then, by first accepting you, yourself, your
being, *with* your negative traits are you likely to be in the
proper mood, and have enough energies, to change those
traits. And the more you castigate yourself for inefficiency, the more inefficient you will most probably
become.

Self-downing, moreover, frequently leads to the other
side of the coin of personal insecurity: compulsive ego-
bolstering. If you think you're no damned good, as a person, because you do foolish or erroneous things, you will
frequently be driven to prove that you really *are* worthwhile; and the way that you will usually try to do this is
by doing presumably ego-inflating things and patting
yourself endlessly on the back for doing them. Thus, if
you can't accept yourself with your undisciplined ways,
you may tend to talk too much, or work compulsively, or
be the life-of-the-party type—in order to impress others
with your good points and thereby deflect them (and
yourself) from seeing what a rotter you really are.

Attempts at ego-inflation are probably as common and
as sabotaging of organizational efficiency as any kind of
other disturbed behavior is. For an executive, in particu-

lar, would better make his decisions and do what he has to do mainly on the basis of whether the activity at hand is likely to benefit him and his concern, and not on the basis of how great he is going to feel ego-wise if this activity succeeds. If he mainly does things to pat himself, or to have others pat him, on the back, he will rarely do them in an effective, no-nonsense-about-it manner. Moreover, he will not be able to admit his errors and do his best to correct them if he has to keep bolstering his self-esteem by pretending that he never really makes serious errors, or that there are special reasons for making them. Again, if he is in dire need of the accolades of others, in order to feel that he is really a great guy and that he deserves to be rewarded in life, he will tend to let these others, including those below him, push him around, get away with murder, or fail to heed his directives. Given the choice of showing how great and beloved he is or getting things done with dispatch and effectiveness, he will almost invariably choose the latter over the former. Otherwise, he largely remains an "executive" in name only.

But isn't it true that a powerful ego-drive is one of the main motivations to executive achievement and that the individual who thinks he *has* to get to the top, in order to show what a worthwhile person he is, stands a better chance of getting there than the individual who is not highly motivated to prove himself and to show that he is "better" than others? Yes and no. Undoubtedly, a good many people have pushed back frontiers and built powerful organizational structures because they were certain that they would thereby win for themselves a place in the sun. They couldn't picture themselves as worthy people *without* this kind of heavenly backing.

But!—most of the people who succeeded for that kind of reason probably got through in spite of, and not necessarily because of, their ego hang-ups. Ten or twenty times their number of highly capable individuals, with the same kind of self-rating disturbances, fell by the wayside and never succeeded at anything because they were too perfectionistic, too anxious, too desperate to work at anything well. Many of them, in fact, copped out completely—killed themselves with alcohol, for example, or became civil service workers—mainly because they couldn't bear to continue to function in an executive capacity when they so desperately *had to* succeed.

Secondly, people who achieve great executive goals for egotistic reasons usually do so at too high a cost. They are continually upset, they do not do well in their human relationships, they are still unhappy after they are "successful," and they sometimes achieve goals (such as the building of Hitler's Third Reich) which are of dubious value. Motivating, indeed, their egocentricity may be; but is the flaming game they play really worth the candle?

In any event, the effective executive would better be self-accepting without being self-rating. He would best aim at assertion (that is, unapologetically going after what he wants to get out of life) without concomitant hostility or aggression (that is, cruelly putting others down, or degrading them as individuals, when they have different views or goals than his own). And how is he to achieve these ends? By getting rid of, or at least minimizing, the two enormous blocks of self-acceptance that most of us—yes, most of us; indeed perhaps almost all of us—have: namely, the inordinate needs to do well and to win the approval of others, and to "prove" to ourselves (and to everyone else) that we are truly great individuals. Let me illustrate.

Bill B. was the president of one of the youngest but most aggressive data-processing companies in his field. In spite of his youth (he was only twenty-nine), he had been able, after originally being a college dropout, to do remarkably well as a programmer, to start his own company in conjunction with two of his friends, and then to take almost complete charge of the company. No one doubted that he was an exceptionally capable, hard-working, energetic individual who could always be counted upon to jump in, especially in times of crisis, and turn a seemingly disastrous turn of events into a sometimes great victory.

Bill, however, was perceptive enough to know some of his own limitations; and when he came to one of the workshops for executives and leaders held by the Institute for Rational Living, he shilly-shallied around, at first, about presenting some of his own problems (though he was very quick and alert in trying to help the other members of the group with theirs), and then finally brought out the thing that was troubling him most. In spite of his unusual achievements, he said, and in spite of the fact that so many others (many of them considerably older and wealthier than he) respected and admired him immensely, he really felt that most people hated his guts and he inwardly turned to jelly (though he maintained a strong outward appearance) whenever he had to make almost any kind of presentation before a group of his peers.

The Activating Event (A) in Bill B's case was rarely anything noxious or frustrating. He almost always succeeded at everything he did—including his social life, where he was frequently the life of the party (albeit after a few drinks). But whenever a situation presented itself where he possibly *might* fail—or at least fail to do perfectly well—he immediately became terribly anxious and began to feel that he was really inadequate, that he was merely fooling most of the people most of the time, and that if his associates and friends truly knew what he was like they would lose all respect for him and probably cut him dead. So A, the Activating Event, was any situation in which Bill *might* not do too well, including all kinds of business and social situations in which, in the final analysis, he invariably succeeded.

C, the emotional Consequence, was Bill's feelings of worthlessness. Curiously enough, he did not even have a large amount of work-confidence or love-confidence, in spite of the fact that he kept performing beautifully in the areas of achievement and popularity. For even when he knew almost for a certainty that he could put through the current business deal on which he was working and even when he was well aware of the fact that the people around him truly seemed to like him and kept saying nice things to him, he felt that there was something essentially rotten about himself and that he was a real phony.

At B, his Belief System, Bill first had the usual kind of rational Belief—and this quickly became apparent when he spoke up at the Institute's executive workshop. In his own words, he kept telling himself: "Considering that I have done so well so far in most of the things I have tried in life, and considering that so many people seem to like and respect me for having done these things, it would be most distressing if I screwed up on this particular deal that is coming up and they then realized that I wasn't so hot after all and that they had made a serious mistake in looking up to me."

This was a perfectly sane and rational Belief, on Bill's part, because there *would* have been distinct negative repercussions if he bolixed up one of the large-scale deals which he usually had on the fire. For the people he associated with would then (1) lose some amount of confidence in his almost sure-fire ability to pull off profitable arrangements, (2) stop putting up the kind of money he usually needed to carry through with these deals, (3) withdraw from some of the other ventures he ran with which they were associated, (4) stop inviting him to some of the high-society gatherings which he delighted to attend, (5) be less likely to introduce him to the very attractive and intelligent girls he liked to date, and (6) withhold various other benefits that they usually were eager to help him obtain. So not only would Bill's theoretical *status* fall in these people's eyes if he started to do badly in his wheeling and dealing, but he would suffer real disadvantages along with the loss of that status.

Bill admitted, when questioned by me and other executives participating in the workshop, that, if he rigorously stuck with his rational Belief about the possibility of his failing in some important situation, he would feel "very disappointed and really concerned." But his *additional* feeling was, he acknowledged, one of extreme anxiety and self-deprecation. The problem was: What *irrational* Beliefs was he vehemently communicating to himself to cause *that* feeling?

Some questioning by me and by the members of the workshop soon brought out Bill's irrational Beliefs. They largely were: "It would be utterly horrible if I bolixed up this particular deal, now that I have done so well in the past and all these people rely on me to keep doing just as well right now. I just couldn't bear to have them see how inept I really am, even though I make such a beautiful surface impression. Once they saw that, I never could join in *any* deals with them again. And if I did, I am sure that I would louse up *all* of them. What a crumb I really am, to give people this phony impression of competence, as I do, when I am quite capable of screwing up everything, and when I feel so inadequate and jellylike inside. How could I be such a hypocrite and imposter!"

The workshop members and I then went on to try to induce Bill to actively challenge and Dispute these irrational ideas. At first, we had great difficulty with him in this respect. For when we asked him, "Would it be utterly horrible if you bolixed up this particular deal, thereby disappointing and disillusioning all the people who rely on you because of your past successes?" he answered: "But of course it would be! Not merely because *I* would lose out, or because they would consider *me* a skunk for having misled them into thinking that I was a marvelous wheeler and dealer. I could probably tolerate that. Because I would realize that they were right in losing faith in me, and probably shouldn't even have had it in the first place. But what about *them*. Quite innocently, they would be misled by me, and headed for a great fall only because of my hypocrisy and my incompetence. Wouldn't it be horrible that *they* would have been hurt thereby?"

We then showed Bill, at point D, how to Dispute his irrational Beliefs, since in his own attempts to Dispute them he was actually adding to them and not challenging them in any real way. The main kinds of Disputing that the workshop members suggested, and that he finally began to go along with, were these:

Question: "Why would it be horrible if you bolixed up this particular deal and thereby disappointed and dis-illusioned all the people who rely on you because of your past successes?" Answer: "It would not be horrible, though it would be unfortunate. Yes, the people who come into this deal with me may well assume that just be-cause I've had past successes that I have to succeed in this one; and they therefore might be terribly disap-pointed and disillusioned, and even hate my guts because I disappointed them. So be it. But if they want to put *me*, as a human being, down because they falsely believe (1) that I *should* succeed again because I have succeeded in the past and (2) that I am a *louse* for performing a *lousy act,* that's their problem. They are thinking quite crook-edly. I certainly don't have to *agree* with their judgment of me. *I* can always accept *myself,* no matter what *they* think of me."

Question: "Why couldn't I bear to have the people I am dealing with see how inept I really am, even though I make such a beautiful surface impression?" Response: "I could bear it. In fact, I could live quite happily, if I chose to do so, even if I continued to be inept or even if they thought I was inept when I really was not. I definitely wouldn't *like* their seeing my ineptitude; but I could *tolerate* it nicely, as long as I didn't falsely tie it up with my being a thoroughly inept *person* and as long as I didn't condemn myself for having this trait and for previously hiding it from people."

Question: "Where is the proof that, once my business associates saw that I didn't pull off this present deal, I could never join in *any* deals with them again, or that if I did so I would louse up *all* of them?" Reply: "There isn't any such evidence, of course. It could be *more difficult* for me to join in with them on future deals, because they perhaps then wouldn't trust me too much. But *difficult* doesn't mean *impossible*. And just because I loused up *this* deal hardly means that I would louse up future ones. In fact, by the experience I received with this one, I could well become *less* prone to mess up future deals. I hardly need a *perfect* record of wheeling and dealing in order to carry off this present deal successfully."

Question: "What makes me a crumb if I give people a phony impression of competence when I am really capable of screwing up everything, and when I feel so inadequate and jellylike inside? Why am I then a hypocrite and impostor?" Rejoinder: "Even if my *behavior* is crumby and phony, I am not *a* crumb or *a* phony. I am merely a human being who *sometimes* acts crumbily and phonily, and who would better try to change this undesirable behavior. But even if I *always* acted in a phony manner, I would not be a crumb; I would simply be a fallible human being, who unfortunately acted in this manner. The mere fact, moreover, that I give people a phony impression of competence does not mean that I am a hypocrite and an impostor, because in the society in which I live it would be pretty unwise—especially for business purposes—to let them know all my weaknesses. As long as *I* admit these weaknesses to myself, I am merely a good game player when I refrain from revealing them to others—just as I would be a good poker player if I had a poor hand and bluffed my opponents into thinking that I had a good one and got them to drop out of the round. It is too bad that, in the kind of world in which I live, I cannot honestly reveal my weaknesses to others and still do very well in business. But if that's the way it is, that's the way it is; and I'd better realistically accept that fact and wisely act accordingly."

When I and the members of Bill's executive workshop group got him to challenge his own irrational Beliefs in this manner, he immediately began to feel better. For he began to accept the fact that, no matter how well he actually did in his business affairs, he also was quite capable of doing very poorly; that his worth as a human being did not depend on whether he achieved magnificently or not; and that even if people were disappointed in any of his performances and thought that he was a fraud, he didn't have to accept their opinion of him and make it their own. It was also significant that, as we worked with Bill, at least a half dozen other high-powered executives kept empathically nodding their heads, as they felt with him his lack of confidence in himself; and it was obvious that, though practically all of them were eminently successful in their work and some of them headed very large organizations, they felt just about the same kind of worthlessness that he felt. Some of them did their best to help him Dispute his irrational Beliefs; and, again, it could be seen that in the process of this Disputing, they were simultaneously helping themselves to challenge their foolish hypotheses about their value as human beings.

This does not mean, again, that executives should not be somewhat meticulous and even perfectionistic about their *work*. The more energy they give to their performances, and the more they correct themselves so that they perform better, the better they are likely to be at their tasks and the higher positions they will tend to attain. There is nothing essentially wrong with this kind of perfectionism.

The problem is that the True Perfectionist insists that not only his performances would better be good but that *he,* a human being, has to prove *his* outstanding value *by* these efforts. He is thus a self-perfectionist rather than merely a work-perfectionist; and although the latter may be rewarding the former tends to be anxiety-provoking and debilitating. Moreover, he almost always becomes idealistic about his anxieties, damns himself for having them, and thereby significantly exacerbates his original difficulties.

This is what happened with Bill. Once he perceived himself as being unconfident and anxious, he put himself down for having these symptoms, and irrationally said to himself: "Hell! Not only do others fail to perceive me as I really am, but *I* know that I come across too well to them and *I* know that I'm anxious about their finding out how rotten I truly am. Now, if I were really a good person, how could I possibly be so anxious? Who ever heard of an insecure organizer of new enterprises? The very essence of good promotional ability is to be decisive and self-confident. And I'm such a ninny underneath! Even if other people never find this out, how can *I* live with this picture of myself?"

When the workshop group got after Bill about his negative attitudes toward himself and his super-negative attitudes about his having the original self-condemning attitudes, he finally was able to say to us: "I've really learned a revolutionary thing at this workshop—something I never came here for and never expected to find out. I thought you would help me solve some of my practical problems—meaning, how to fool others better and keep promoting my deals in spite of my terrible anxieties. I now see that I'm doing pretty well at that sort of thing, and that maybe I could teach all of you a lesson in that respect!

"But the really new thing I've learned is that I don't have to have any *image* of myself at all. I can be me— can exist, try to succeed at what I want to do, and look for the things I really enjoy in life—without making up *images*. What do I need *pictures* of me for, anyway? Whatever the hell my *picture* looks like, or how I get it retouched and how I impress others by showing it to them, does that *really* make *me* any different?"

"What do you mean *you?*" one of the other executives in the workshop asked. "What are *you,* anyway?"

"I'm not entirely sure," Bill answered, "but at least I

see that I'm not any goddamned *picture!* I suppose that *I* am the things I really like to do—because *I* truly like to do them. I am my desires for rare roast beef, well-built women who are a little overweight (like my wife), and wheeling and dealing—which I enjoy a lot. I am many other things I like, some of which I'm not even certain of what they are yet, but I sure intend to find out. But whatever *I* am, whatever my desires are, I hope to stop making up images, pictures of what I *should* be, and then pretending that I actually am those images. I'm not sure, yet, since I just learned this information in the last couple of hours and have not thoroughly assimilated it and begun to use it too much, whether I'll finally completely give up those blasted images. But I damned well am going to try!"

Again, many of the heads of the other executives at the workshop nodded in unison. They, too, had largely come to have me help them with their practical organizational problems. But they now were beginning to see that their problems *about themselves* were the real issues, and that if they could thoroughly accept their own limitations, and give up having to impress others with their *images,* they had enough education, training, experience, and brain-power to figure out most of the practical answers for themselves.

9 Overcoming feelings
of hostility

Self-assertion is one of the healthiest
goals imaginable, and one that is likely to help you become and remain an efficient executive. But it is all too
easy to confuse self-assertion and hostility—as even some
of the best-trained professionals in the field of psychology
do. For many people find that, in order for them to make
themselves assertive, and to really stand up for what they
want, they first have to make themselves enraged at others for not easily and quickly giving them what they desire. Because their hostility or anger impels them to be
assertive, and sometimes to achieve good (or at least
quick) results, they wrongly conclude that (1) it is
necessary for assertion, (2) it is a show of strength, (3)

it is a correct statement about what is going on in the world, and (4) it is a highly desirable feeling.

Assertion is healthy because it states that you want something and that you are determined to do something about getting this want satisfied, even though some of the people you are involved with have different preferences and would much rather you'd do what they wanted.

Hostility is quite another thing. You hate your wife for insisting on eating in cheaper rather than in finer restaurants. You loathe your sister for being addicted to musical comedies. You bitterly resent the other executives in your company who are trying to be president and who want to keep you at the vice-president level. In these instances, you are not merely striving to get what you want; you are downing, as human beings, those who want something else than you do. You are insisting that you feel a certain way about things and that others *therefore* should feel the same way you do. But you do not run the universe; and there is no reason whatever that other people should go along for your ride.

Your hostility, consequently, does not stem from their differences with or even opposition to you. It is caused by your refusal to accept those differences and that opposition and by your trying to *dictate* that everything go exactly the way you want it to go. If you would keep your desire but surrender your dictatorial attitude, you would still have your own point of view, and you might well strongly assert yourself to have it fulfilled. But you would not feel exceptionally hostile toward those who did not immediately and fully go along with your viewpoint.

Lack of hostility is particularly desirable for you, as an

executive, because otherwise your anger will frequently block your way no matter how good are your goals and how intelligently you are trying to pursue them. This is notably true in regard to your hostility against higher-ups in your organization. For if you hate your immediate boss or one of the officers of your company, either you will tend to communicate this feeling to him—which won't be very good for you!—or else you will keep it to yourself, and perhaps produce an ulcer—which also won't be very good!

This means that you would better accept the fact that your superiors are not angels, and that instead they are frequently disturbed or peculiar in various ways; that you can expect them to do many wrong, stupid things; that no matter what their errors are, you would best either ignore them or bring them tactfully to their attention. Just the fact that you are efficient—and let us suppose that you are—is no good reason for you to demand that everyone else in your organization, including the higher-ups, be equally competent and capable. And even when, by their foolishness or their lack of ability, they prevent you from acting the way you would like to act and from advancing as much as you would like to advance, that's tough! But that's the way of the world, and often there is nothing reconstructive, particularly in the short run, that you can do about it.

This is often even truer for a good many of the people who work on your level or under you. It cannot exactly be said that all employees are incompetent or goofing. Not *exactly;* but very largely! I'll never forget the days of World War II. We, in the United States, were engaged in what seemed to be a life-or-death struggle with two of the most ruthless and efficient powers, Germany and Japan, that ever existed on this earth. Almost everyone in our country was fairly enthusiastically in favor of the war, since we considered our enemies unwarranted aggressors and felt that we were saving the world from their murderous depredations. We also knew that these two war machines were well supplied and well oiled and that only unusual productive efficiency on our part would be likely to enable us to win on the battlefields. We consequently put huge amounts of publicity into alerting ourselves to the desirability of working hard, saving metal, keeping our lights dim, refraining from changing jobs, and otherwise contributing to the war effort. Almost everyone in the country, including the left-wing radicals of the day, agreed with these goals and supposedly did his best to support them. And what happened?

Very little, as far as efficiency is concerned. From the stories told to me by my clients—many of whom worked in war-connected industries—shirking, procrastination, lateness, profit-mulcting, and similar forms of sabotaging were rampant, among almost everyone, from the lowliest workers to the highest executives. From my own observations, I concluded then (and still believe today) that the main reason we won the war was not because of our marvelous productivity (which we kept boasting about ad nauseam) but because we, by sheer luck, happened to have two or three times the amount of natural resources (land, food, important mineral deposits, etc.) and of manpower as did our enemies. And even at that, we came perilously close to losing on a few occasions.

What is the main point I am making here? That almost all human beings naturally find it easy to be slothful, goofing, sidetracking, and ineffectual. Therefore, if you really want to be an efficient executive and to avoid becoming continually angry and upset, you'd better face that reality. Occasionally, you will encounter in your organizational work a superior or a subordinate who loves his work, who responsibly pursues it at virtually all times, and who helps rather than sabotages much of your activity. Occasionally! Most of the time, you will meet people in quite the opposite camp.

I say this because I can honestly face my own deficiencies in this respect when I was in the business world. For ten years, while I was gathering material for some of my future books and while I was obtaining my Ph.D. degree in clinical psychology, I worked for a moderately large gift and novelty wholesale house. I started as a typist and file clerk (who also ran errands and swept the floor) and ended up as the personnel manager (and, unofficially, as the vice president). During this decade, I was probably one of the most efficient men in the business and perhaps the firm's main contributor to its outstanding success; since I did my work beautifully and devised bookkeeping, billing, filing, mail order, and other systems which helped the firm enormously and saved literally hundreds of hours of time a year for the president, who was then able to devote his efforts to building up sales.

At the same time, if I am to be ruthlessly honest with myself, I have to admit that I took as much of the firm's time as I possibly could (for which I was being paid very well) to do my own work, including a great deal of work on my Ph.D. dissertation; that I shamelessly exploited my connections with the business, sometimes to its detriment; that I overbilled it for expenses and overtime on many occasions; that at one time I unfairly tried to set up a business that directly competed with it; and that I committed various other dubiously ethical acts during all the years that I worked for it. And I, mind you, was an unusually diligent, unprocrastinating, reliable, competent employee!

The point I am making, if perhaps a little verbosely, is that even the most effective organization people have their serious flaws and tricks. I have them; and everyone I have ever worked with has had them. If you, therefore, want to be an efficient executive, and especially to get along with your associates in an unhostile manner, you'd better acknowledge this fact and stop expecting humans to be superhuman. It's often unfortunate that just about all of them are, as Nietzsche wisely observed a good many years ago, human all too human; but if that's the way they are, then that's the way they are.

Let's take a concrete example, to show you how you can refrain from feeling—let alone acting—angry and resentful even when some of your associates are obviously behaving badly. Let us assume—at point A—that your immediate superior, Mr. Richards, is jealous of your energy and intelligence (because he, let us say, is not in your class in these respects, and probably never will be) and that therefore he deliberately puts various blocks in your way. You are a conscientious executive, so normally you take on more than your share of the work and usually compensate for his interference and manage to get your work done and keep up the reputation of your department. At the same time, you have a new assistant, who happens to be the son-in-law of the president of your outfit, who not only is so incompetent that he would have never got the job without the president's nepotism, but who also comes in late regularly, does very little actual work, and curries favor with Mr. Richards and sometimes seems to be scheming with him against you.

At point A, the Activating Experience, you are therefore getting more than your share of trouble. At point B, your Belief System, you have the perfectly rational Belief: "What bad luck! Of all the people for whom I could be working, it had to be Richards! It's bad enough getting along with the average person they put over you in this kind of an outfit. But working with him—wow! He's so damned prejudiced against me, probably because of his jealousy of me, that I hardly have a chance to please him. Then, to make matters worse, there's my so-called assistant. Assistant, my eye! He assists me in getting into trouble with Richards, and in very few other ways! I might expect to have some incompetent family member hanging on my neck in a concern like this; but, boy, does he abuse the privilege! His coming in late, his poor work habits, and his currying favor with Richards make things miserable around here. What trouble!"

As usual, if you stayed rigorously only with these rational Beliefs, you would feel displeased, disappointed, and even disillusioned with your job. And, as a result of these feelings, you might try to correct conditions, get transferred to another department, or even quit the firm. But you would not be terribly upset, unless you "graduated" or escalated into some clear-cut magical or irrational Belief. Such as? Well: "How the devil could they have put an idiot like *Richards* over me? How terrible that this could have happened to me! It's totally unfair that he is so prejudiced, and things shouldn't *be* that unfair! And my assistant, too! Look how awful he is! How can he treat me that way, when he doesn't have a right to be here in the first place, and when he's acting so irresponsibly in the second place? What a horrible situation!"

It is these irrational Beliefs, at point B, and not the unpleasant Activating Events you are experiencing, at point A, that are truly making you feel upset and angry. And although these Beliefs, on the surface, may seem entirely logical and warranted, they really have nothing to do with reality. For they stem from your exaggerated *evaluations* of the facts of your life, and not from these facts themselves.

How would you go about Disputing and challenging your own crazy Beliefs, at point D? Something like this:

Question: "How could they have put an idiot like Richards over me?" Answer: "They easily could! People who behave the way Richards does are frequently placed in charge of people who behave the way I do. That's the way the world is: full of situations like this. Why should *I* be an exception to the general rule that Richards acts the way Richards acts, and that individuals who act this way are often put in a supervisory position over individuals who act more intelligently and sanely?"

Question: "Why is it terrible that this could have happened to me?" Response: "It's only terrible because I *think* it's terrible. Naturally, I don't like it. I never will. But why can't I stand what I don't like? I can! If I really don't like it *enough,* then I don't have to work for my present company at all. I do have the choice of quitting. But if I think *I* can get more out of staying than quitting, I'd better take the disadvantages of staying—namely, that people like Richards (and my assistant) will be around to bother me, and that the company has every right to have them around. That's certainly a pain in the ass; but it's hardly *terrible.*"

Question: "Where is the evidence that things shouldn't be so unfair, and that Richards shouldn't be prejudiced against me?" Reply: "There isn't any evidence. There are lots of unfair things in the world, and the fact that Richards is so prejudiced against me is one of them. But unfairness exists; it is one of the main facts of life; and he has a perfect right to be as unfair as he is, just as I have a right to try to induce him not to be. But if I fail to persuade him to be fair, then I fail. Why *must* I succeed in getting everybody to treat me fairly? Obviously, there is no reason why I must."

Question: "Why is my assistant awful? Why can he not treat me the way he does, even though he is only here because he's related to the president?" Answer: "He is not an awful person; merely a person who acts very badly toward *me.* Even if I could prove that he acted irresponsibly toward everyone, I still couldn't show that he was a bad *individual.* For if an individual is bad or awful, that means that he can *never* do any good things and that he deserves to be damned for constantly doing bad ones. Well, how can I prove that he could *never* do any good things? And even if I could, why would he then deserve to be doomed to perdition for acting in that manner? On the contrary, if he really is as hopelessly bad in all his performances as I am claiming that he is, then he probably deserves to be helped and protected rather than to be damned. I'll never like his treating me the way he does, and making my working life more difficult; but he obviously *can* treat me that way in spite of the fact that he got his job through his relationship with the president of our company and not by anything effective he has done. His getting the job in this manner has nothing to do with the way he can or cannot treat me. Even if he were the worst worker imaginable, he would still be able to treat me poorly. In fact, the poorer he is at his job and the less deserving of holding it (by the usual kinds of company standards) the more likely it is that he *will* treat me badly—for that's the way those who work poorly frequently treat their superiors. Well, if that's the way he behaves, that's it; and why don't I accept the reality of it's being that way?"

Question: "What makes my situation so horrible?" Answer: "Nothing does; or, rather, *I* do. The situation is certainly not very beneficial or advantageous. In fact, it is downright *dis*advantageous! But merely because my environmental circumstances are *undesirable* does not make them *horrible*. Undesirability clearly exists: What I do not want, I almost automatically find undesirable. But *horror* is a fiction, a myth, a demon that I invent. It doesn't merely mean *very* undesirable. It means that I find my situation impossible and intolerable *because* it is undesirable. But *impossible* and *intolerable* are fabrications, which have nothing to do with reality. For it is obviously *possible* for me to be in this undesirable situation; and I clearly can *tolerate* being in it (even though I may choose not to do so and may quit my job because I so choose). So I'd better face the facts—which are bad enough—without making them worse than they are in my fictionalizing head. Sure I find the situation undesirable; and I'm never likely to find it desirable. O.K., so it's what I don't desire. So are hundreds of other situations I encounter in life. Now, my main sensible choices are: (1) Find a way to change it and make it more desirable; (2) Get out of it; (3) gracefully accept it the way it is. Which one of these choices am I going to focus on and try to work out?"

Your hostility, in other words, does not stem (as you wrongly think it does) from the poor behavior of your organizational associates. Rather, it originates in your puerile reactions—or overreactions—to their presumably poor behavior. Frequently you have as much chance of changing them and their undesirable activities as you have of ruling the universe. And that's exactly what, by making yourself resentful and angry, you are really trying to do: rule the world. You are dictating and demanding that someone whom you definitely do not control be absolutely controllable by you. And when he proves not to be, you inwardly or outwardly rant—and make another silly assumption thereby—that your ranting will change him. Then, when it doesn't, you frequently go on to demand: "That son of a bitch *should* change! There *ought to be* something I can do to make him behave differently! He's no damned good for acting the way he does and then having the gall to remain that way when I am so displeased by his behavior and when I make such great efforts to change him!"

So you go round and round. You demand that So-and-so treat you well, and you make yourself terribly upset when he doesn't. Then you dictate that he must listen to your angry tirades against him, and you make yourself still angrier when he doesn't. Then you anger yourself at your own ineptness in getting him to treat you fairly or to listen to your tirades. By this time, you have at least three—and perhaps more—levels of self-created anger; and you can go on to augment these levels almost indefinitely.

Palliatively, you try several things. You tell off some of the people you are angry at, and let them know exactly what you think of them. You pound a pillow or a punching bag, while imagining that it is really the head of your frustrating superior or subordinate. You go to some anger-encouraging encounter groups and scream and whine about how awful people are to you and what shits some of the other members of the groups are. You become addicted to blood-and-thunder movies, to bloody prize fights, or to gory war novels. Sometimes, after "releasing" your anger in these ways, you feel absolutely great. Momentarily. For you have temporarily, in some actual or symbolic way, put someone else down, and you feel nobler and superior to him and think of yourself as "stronger" or "greater." How nice, how ego-inflated you feel!

Crap! You still have the two-year-old's philosophy you previously held; and maybe now believe it even a little

stronger! For as you are telling people off, pounding pil-
lows, whining to your encounter group about them, or
seeing them as the villains of movies or novels, you are
still mostly convincing yourself: "Take that, you worm!
You *are* no good! I hate you! You really deserve to die
for the cruel way you are treating me! You lousy
bastard!" And your self-statements are utter balderdash,
no matter how great they make you feel. For the person
you are foaming and fuming against is *not* a worm—but
only a fallible, and at times quite possibly unethical and
unfair, human being. He *isn't* worthless—though some of
his acts toward you may be reprehensible. If you hate
him, rather than some of his behavior, you are damning
him as a total human being—which is inaccurate and unfair on your part. He doesn't deserve to die, but at most
to be restrained or restricted, if he is actually treating you
cruelly. And he isn't a lousy bastard—but, again, at
worst a human being with weaknesses and errors.

So you may well *feel* better after you have put yourself
fully in touch with your angry emotions and violently let
them out, in some direct or indirect manner; but it is
doubtful if you will *get* better under these conditions. For
getting better, or becoming less seriously disturbed, almost invariably involves growing up, thinking straighter,
and figuring out a method of reacting sanely to others on
the basis of facts and reality rather than on the basis of
silly fictions in your head.

This doesn't mean that your *anger* is a fiction. On the
contrary, it is a definite reality, and would better be fully
acknowledged by you as one of the most real feelings
that you have. But the ideas with which you create it—

especially the notions that people *must* treat you fairly and that they are complete *lice* when they do not—are foolish fantasies, and fantasies which usually do much more harm than good.

Organizational activity, on the other hand, is usually as down-to-earth and nonmystical as any human activity can be. The more phantomlike it becomes, the less it is likely to survive. As even some of the screwiest people seem to "intuitively" know.

Like the branch manager of one of the major health publishing organizations who came to a workshop for executives which the Institute for Rational Living sponsored at its New York headquarters. This woman was so disorganized in her social life that it was interfering with her business efficiency, and she mainly wanted to make a better social adjustment so she would have the time and energies to settle down to a more peaceful managerial existence. But staying out very late most nights, nursing a broken heart every few weeks, and overdrinking herself into a state of obesity which conflicted with all the ideals her organization was trying to foster were doing her work at the office no good whatever.

Curiously enough, she was surprisingly responsible in the work she did take on, and she knew there was some inconsistency about this responsibility and her dramatic lack of responsibility to herself in her social life. "How come," she asked, "I am so good at work—getting there on time, keeping all my appointments, turning in my reports, never really trying to get away with anything—and at the same time I am so procrastinating and lax in so many other things I do?"

"There's probably a simple answer to that question," I replied. "You're a bright woman, and you know perfectly well that if you acted at the office in any way like you act in the rest of your life, you just couldn't get by for very long. For what outfit is going to put up with continual lateness, copping out on appointments, failing to turn in reports, and other kinds of procrastination and laxness? Not yours, I'm sure! While after office hours, on the other hand, it's not very hard for you to pick companions who *will* let you get away with this kind of behavior—particularly when they're men who want to get into your pants and who are willing to put up with a number of hassles and bad behavior on your part to accomplish that end. But businesses invariably require some kind of *re-sults*—such as more profit and less loss. And unless you can show your central office that you are getting such results, and are toeing some kind of businesslike mark to get them, how long are they going to keep you around? So you can make up all kinds of excuses and stories when you don't show up for your date with Joe on Friday and suddenly turn up, unannounced, at his apartment on Saturday. But what *business* venture is going to put up with that kind of inconsistency?"

In the final analysis, as well as to a great degree in the shorter run, organizational work is based on figures, facts, results, and dollars. Hopeful fantasies may get some aspect of it going; but to continue, hard-headed reality must eventually have its day and its way. When you *observe*, therefore, that your boss's behavior is unfair, stupid, or execrable, that is one thing. But when you *imagine* that he has horns and a tail for engaging in that kind of behavior, that is another thing entirely! Your observations about the unfortunate deeds of your associates may be perceptive and real, and may hold you in good stead. But your *dreaming up* that they are ogres, vermin, skunks, and no-goodniks for performing these deeds will only lead to hostile feelings in your gut—and, usually, to sabotaging still further your relations with them.

10 Conquering depression

It is almost phenomenal how many individuals, including those in the highest executive brackets, are fairly steadily plagued by feelings of depression. This is also true of some of the most outstanding artists, writers, and composers, too—as witness the cases of Beethoven, Leonardo, and Michelangelo—all of whom spent considerable periods of their lives in rather acutely depressed states.

Not that depression adds to productivity. On the contrary! Even the most capable organizer or activist, once he succumbs to a state of melancholia, tends to become listless, inert, tired, procrastinating, and nonperforming. As usual, moreover, the picture in connection with this kind of emotional disturbance becomes complicated by the secondary symptoms. Noting that he is unalert, depressed, and bogged down, the normally productive executive becomes exceptionally morose *because* of this depression—becomes depressed about being depressed. Then things get even worse, and the vicious circle becomes a veritable vortex of despair.

Are there many different kinds of irrational ideas that lead to depression or just a few? Usually, surprisingly few. Take, typically, the case of Charlie K., a client who came to see me some time ago because he was severely depressed, was unaffected by the antidepressants he was gulping by the mouthful, and was referred by his internist, who had himself seen me some years before when he was in a fit of depression and had been helped to overcome it.

Charlie did indeed have real business problems, so there seemingly was nothing strange about his state of despondency. He was the founder and president of a fairly large organization which, mainly because of poor conditions in the industry, was not in the best of shape. His main helper, and the vice president of the company, had recently had a heart attack, and would not be back in full action for a few months. His second main assistant, on whom he now had to rely more than ever, was dissatisfied with his position (largely because he was jealous of the ill vice president) and might quit at any moment. His eighteen-year-old son was failing at college, and had just been put on probation.

So Charlie certainly had his problems! And everyone.

including his sympathetic wife, thought he had every reason to be depressed. Everyone except me. "Look," I said, when I first saw him for a few psychotherapy sessions, "there's no doubt that several things are bad in your life —business conditions, your vice president's heart attack, the dissatisfaction of this other fellow on whom you have to rely right now, and your son's being put on probation at school. All these things stink; they're unpleasant; there is no reason you should like them. But they're merely Activating Events or Experiences—which I call point A, in my system. And these unfortunate Activating Experiences, at A, come before, or activate, the feelings or Consequences, which you have, at point C. But the events at A really do not cause the Consequences or feelings at C. Because if a hundred executives in your position all experienced, at A, your present difficulties, they would not all feel equally depressed, as you are feeling, at point C. What Consequences do you think most of them would feel at C?"

"Well, I suppose most of them would feel anxious or upset."

"Yes, you're probably right. Most of them probably would feel anxious or upset, at C, after they experienced poor business conditions, a heart attack that incapacitated their vice president, the dissatisfaction of their other main assistant, and their son being put on probation, at point A. But actually, if they rigorously stuck to appropriate reactions at what I call B, their Belief System, if they *only* convinced themselves, at B, 'This is really unfortunate; I don't like it; what a hell of a bother;

I wish these lousy events had not occurred,' what Consequences or feelings do you think they would then experience, at C?"

"Mmm. Let's see. I guess they would feel disappointed and troubled."

"Right! They would feel disappointed, because they were not getting what they wanted. And they would feel troubled, because they would wonder what they could do to change the obnoxious Activating Experiences, at point A, and would not immediately come up with any great solutions. But feelings of disappointment and of being troubled, at C, are not the same as feelings of anxiety and depression, which you seem to have and which many people would have, at C. Are they?"

"No, I guess they're not," said Charlie.

"No, they're not. There consequently are some *other* things they are convincing themselves, at point B, to *create* feelings of anxiety and depression, at point C. And where it is perfectly appropriate and rational for them to be telling themselves, 'How unfortunate! I don't like what is occurring at A. What a pain in the ass!' and thereby to make themselves feel disappointed and troubled—and, at the same time, to spur themselves, by such feelings, to work at *changing* the Activating Events at A if they can possibly do so—it is, according to my theory, highly inappropriate and irrational for them to be telling themselves these *other* ideas that they are convincing themselves of, at B, to make themselves feel anxious and depressed. Now what do you think the irrational Beliefs are that they—and you—are powerfully convincing yourself at point B?"

"Mmmm. I guess they're saying something like, 'I failed. If I had only done things better, I wouldn't be in this position. But I didn't.' "

"Yes," I said. "They frequently are convincing themselves that they failed. But that's just an *observation*. For in a sense, they did. You, for example, failed to pick a business that wouldn't be affected by poor general conditions. You failed to pick a vice president who would remain perfectly healthy. You failed to make your second main assistant satisfied with his job. And you failed to help make your son a good student. So, objectively, you have failed in many ways. But you could accurately *observe* that you have failed and this observation would never, in itself, cause you to *feel* anything. According to the principles of Rational Sensitivity—which are based on extensive psychological experimentation and clinical findings—you also have a *conclusion* about your observation of having failed; and it is that conclusion, the irrational one that you have, which upsets you. Now, what do you think that conclusion *about* your failing is?"

"Oh," replied Charlie, "I guess it is, 'And I shouldn't have failed. What an incompetent I am for failing!' "

"Right! That's probably what you are concluding. And those irrational conclusions, among others, are depressing you. You probably have some other irrational conclusions, too. Such as: 'How awful it is for business conditions to be the crummy way they are and for my right-hand man to be out of commission for a few months!' And: 'That goddamned general manager, what an ingrate and a nut he is! After all we've done for him, he idiotically gets jealous of the vice president and now wants to quit us—at a time like this! What a bastard he is!' "

"Yes, I must admit that I have had ideas like that. And he *is* an idiot, if not a bastard; and I do feel it is terrible that he is acting the way he is!"

"Exactly! So those are some of your conclusions or ideas, at B, about what is happening at A; and it is these conclusions, and not the Activating Events at A, that are upsetting you. Now, how could you go on to challenge— to Dispute, at D—your silly conclusions?"

"Well, I guess I could ask myself: 'Why *shouldn't* I have failed?' And: 'How does failing make me a total incompetent?' "

"Yes, those are good questions. And what are the answers?"

"First of all, now that you've made me think about it, I see there really *isn't* any reason why I *shouldn't* have failed. After all, I'm human. And humans fail. I theoretically *could* have gone into a different business, picked another vice president, stopped the general manager from being so jealous, and induced my son to work harder at school. But I didn't. I wasn't omniscient. And there's no reason why I *should* have been."

"No, none at all. Like all humans, you are fallible. You *will* make errors. And, as you're now asking yourself, why shouldn't you continue to be human and to make mistakes? How about your conclusion that you are an incompetent for failing?"

"Well, I *did* act incompetently. At least in part. For one thing, I neglected my relations with the general manager. And I hardly checked to see how my son was doing in school, even though I knew he was the kind of a boy who often gets into academic trouble and who goofs."

"O.K., so you did act incompetently. But does that make you *an* incompetent?"

"No, I guess it doesn't."

"*Why* doesn't it?"

Charlie was stumped for almost a minute. Then he haltingly replied: "Because *an* incompetent would be no good at practically anything. And I do a good many things well, in spite of my failings."

"Right. *An* incompetent would *always* have to be incompetent; and that's hardly your case. Moreover, *an* incompetent is a pejorative term that we use for an individual who not only consistently does poorly but who is to be damned, condemned for doing poorly. It really means, does it not, a *louse?*"

"Yes, I guess you're right. When I think of myself as *an* incompetent, I think of myself as a total slob, a person who deserves to be damned for his incompetence."

"And that is an error, of course. For even if we could prove that you are and would always be incompetent, why should we put you into hell for having the trait of ineptness? If anything, we should then *help* you, give you special assistance—and hardly condemn you for behaving so badly and being, presumably, born to be such a *schnook.*"

"So I can accept myself," Charlie remarked, "with any incompetencies that I may possess."

"Yes, you can. And if you do so, if you accept you, your existence, with your failings, you can then go back to A and try to correct those failings. While if you damn yourself for your errors, you will become so obsessed with your self-flagellation that you will have less time and energy to devote to the correcting process."

"So it's all as simple as that, eh?"

"Yes, but let's consider a few more irrationalities we so far have overlooked. What about your belief that it is awful for business conditions to be the crummy way they are and for your vice president to be out of commission for a few months?"

"Oh, I can see that's nonsense. It's unpleasant, of course, for business to be this way and for him to have had a heart attack at this time. But that's the way it is: unpleasant. And I can live with this unpleasantness and still go about my business, and try to make it good in spite of these two nasty conditions."

"Exactly. And how about your general manager being a bastard? Is that correct?"

"To tell you the truth, I still feel that he is. But I can now see that this feeling is based on the nutty idea that he *shouldn't* be acting the way he is. And, of course, he *should* be, in the sense that he *is*. I pride myself on accepting reality. But I see that, in this respect, I'm definitely not doing this. I'm *insisting* that his behavior be different from the way it is, and of course I can't change it and better not insist that I can. He has every right to act the way he does; and he is not a bastard for acting that way—merely a person whom I think is behaving foolishly. O.K. So that's *his* problem. Now, why can't I accept him with this problem?"

"Right again. It's *unfortunate* that he's acting the way he is; but it's not *terrible*. And he has a right, it is his nature, to do anything he does—even though he behaves quite wrongly. As I have said in my writings, everyone has *a right to be wrong*. For that is the human condition: to keep making errors. And for us to say 'He has no right to be wrong' is really to deprive him of his humanity. He may be wrong for being wrong—mistaken, erroneous, that is—but he has every right to be human and to behave wrongly. It's just too bad that he exerts that right!"

"You know," Charlie said, "I'm already beginning to feel a lot better. I can feel that a real burden has lifted from me. It's almost miraculous! When I came in here, I was extremely depressed and morose. Now I feel almost light-hearted. I only hope I can keep this up!"

"You can," I replied, "if you keep *working* at it. For you can see a thing quickly and easily—like the fact that conditions *are* the way they are and that it isn't awful or catastrophic. But a half hour or a day from now you can easily sink back to your old, deeply ingrained, infinitely human philosophy: 'But they *shouldn't* be that way! It's awful! I can't stand it!' And then you'll begin to feel depressed all over again. But if every single time you feel that way, at point C, you immediately track it down to what's happening at point A—the fact that obnoxious Activating Events exist in your life—and to your irrational Beliefs *about* these events at point B—especially your Beliefs that *it's awful* to be frustrated and mistaken —then you will not only quickly change your emotional Consequence, at C, but after doing it many times you will get to a point where you almost automatically respond differently. Thus, a while from now, when a different series of obnoxious occurrences transpire at point

A, you will be automatically responding to yourself, most of the time, with philosophies such as "Tough shit! That's the way it is. It's unfortunate that the world is so rough, and the people in it are so nutty; but it's only unfortunate, it's not horrible or catastrophic." When you get to this point, you'll rarely upset yourself and make yourself depressed about the very things that you now habitually react to poorly and about which you depress yourself."

"You really think that I can get to that point, after a while?"

"I'm sure you *can;* but I don't know whether you *will.* Anyone who can believe bullshit—that it is awful for things to go wrong in his world and that they absolutely shouldn't be that way—can refuse to believe this same bullshit. Whatever you believe, you can disbelieve. So if you keep *working* at challenging and Disputing your own nonsense, whenever you feel depressed, you will gradually give it up and get to the point of rarely spontaneously believing it again. It's not merely insight into the nonsense that you require, however—it's *practicing* giving it up, giving it up, giving it up, until you've really got yourself over it."

Charlie did work at it. I only saw him for a half dozen individual sessions of psychotherapy, and then he joined one of my groups and participated in group therapy, on a once-a-week basis, for about thirty weeks. He also attended one of the Institute for Rational Living's Workshops for Executives. With this activity, plus reading some of the books and pamphlets on rational-emotive therapy, he was able to help himself considerably and to become undepressed. Several years have passed since that time, and he has not been seriously depressed about anything. And he has managed to pull himself out of several serious scrapes—including the death of the vice president of his company—mainly because he has not consumed too much time and energy in depressing himself.

Does Rational Sensitivity teach people that they need *never* get depressed about anything—even, say, the death of a loved one or the bankruptcy of a business? Yes, it does. For depression does not merely mean, when it is properly defined, great sorrow, sadness, or unhappiness; it also means self-downing, self-pity, and a feeling of utter hopelessness. If you tell yourself, "Isn't it unfortunate that my firm is failing? I am going to be highly disappointed and frustrated if it actually does fail," you will tend to feel extremely sorry and displeased. But to feel depressed, you invariably add other, unvalidatable propositions, such as: "Isn't it awful that my firm is failing? There must be something rotten about me if I cannot stop it from going bankrupt. How can a slob like me possibly go on living happily in a world where such horrible things exist? If it ever goes bankrupt, I'll *never* be able to get another position like this or to make it successfully in this harsh universe!"

For you to be frustrated, inconvenienced, and annoyed naturally encourages you to feel sad and low—though you could, of course, actually convince yourself that it is good to be thus disadvantaged and could actually make yourself feel happy. But for you to feel depressed, despairing, and completely blue means, really, that you are *annoying yourself about being annoyed,* that you are demanding and whining that the world should be arranged so you are never very frustrated, inconvenienced, and annoyed. Depression, like sorrow, is a "natural" result of frustration, and particularly of continued or great frustration. But while it is exceptionally difficult, and very often undesirable, for you to stop feeling sorrowful about noxious Activating Events, it is less difficult and quite desirable for you to stop making yourself depressed.

Rational Sensitivity, therefore, usually encourages you to feel sad and unhappy about the real hassles that you, as an executive or a person, may experience—for it is not in the least opposed to emotion, and in fact favors many appropriate emotions—such as sadness and regret—which motivate you to think about noxious events and to do your best to overcome them and prevent their recurrence. But it does discourage depression and despair—since it holds that these are usually inappropriate emotions that sabotage your effectively dealing with unpleasant life situations and render you less effective as an executive and as an individual.

11 Instant and profound attacks on emotional upsets

Rational Sensitivity is no miracle cure. It works because *you* work it. And it works because it is based on a solid understanding of what so-called human nature is, how it normally results in foolish thinking and inappropriate emoting, and what specifically can be done to change this thinking and hence minimize or eliminate the self-sabotaging emoting. If you have carefully read this book so far, you can see that Rational Sensitivity is an easily understandable, directly attacking method which quickly gets at the main philosophic core of all kinds of emotional upsets and which gives the troubled person an efficient, scientifically based method of uprooting them.

When placed in the A-B-C format of Rational Sensitivity, virtually any person's disturbing or dysfunctional emotional Consequences can be tracked down to their basic ideological sources. They can then be so effectively undermined that they tend to disappear almost immediately. The individual also acquires the tendency to think differently about potentially disturbing Activating Experiences or Activating Events in the future, to take them much less seriously and change his Belief System in regard to them, and therefore to refuse to make himself overconcerned about them. He then is much less upsettable than he was before and tends to become over- or underexcited only rarely.

Is there even a quicker method by which you can understand and undermine your emotional problems and thereby unblock yourself from unnecessary, self-imposed restrictions on your becoming a highly effective executive (and a happier human being)? Yes, there are several such methods—but it takes a whale of a lot of thinking and practicing to put them to good use and to make them, finally, work almost automatically. We shall now, to complete this book on Rational Sensitivity, outline some of these shorter methods.

The first—and perhaps the most efficient—way of unblocking yourself emotionally is for you to use determinedly two of the strongest and most sanity-producing words in the English language—two words which constitute one of the most elegant answers to virtually any conceivable emotional difficulty.

"Do you actually mean to say," you may incredulously ask, "that there are two words which can be easily understood and instantly applied to practically any imaginable emotional upset and that if I use these two words properly, I will no longer suffer from any serious disturbance?"

Well, not exactly. That's putting it a little *too* strongly. For human beings, just because they are human, are almost bound to undergo some kinds of anxieties, depressions, rages, or other psychological difficulties—at least occasionally or intermittently. It's just not realistic to expect them *completely* to stop plaguing themselves emotionally.

"But you imply that *most* of the time, in *nearly* all instances, a person could use two common words and by their use minimize or eliminate the greater part of his hang-ups. Is that correct?"

Definitely. More precisely, I contend that there are two words which people continually employ which cause about 99 percent of their psychological problems; and that there are two other words (which can even, less expressively, be reduced to one) which they could use to undo just about all the neurotic dilemmas which they cause themselves by devout belief in the original two words.

"You must be kidding! Do you seriously mean to say that all the scientific findings and complexities about personality maladjustment which have been discovered over the past several thousand years, and which have been particularly revealed by the intensive analyses of Sigmund Freud, Alfred Adler, Carl Jung, and their many followers, can be accurately summarized in just two words? And that these same complex behavior disorders can then be resolved by the individual who is afflicted with them if he accurately and determinedly employs two other words?"

No, I'm not kidding; and I do mean just that. Of course, these key words I am about to reveal have many variations and several different meanings. And, as you would expect, the individual who employs them may do so in a number of sincere and less sincere, full-hearted and half-hearted ways. So I am not claiming that they are always equally effective or long-lasting in their results. But if properly used (and not cavalierly abused), they will almost invariably do wonders for the emotionally harassed person.

"That sounds much too simple to be true. But I can hardly wait to hear what you have to say. First, what *are* the two words that supposedly cause practically all emotional disturbance?"

They are: "It's awful!" Or, in some other variations, "How horrible!" "My God!" "It's terrible!" "How catastrophic!" Let me illustrate.

Whenever you feel, at what I call point C, the disturbed Consequences of anxiety, depression, worthlessness, or some other self-deprecating feelings, you are almost invariably convincing yourself something like, "*It's awful* that I may not get promoted!" "*It's awful* that my wife no longer loves me!" "*It's awful* that I'm not as efficient an executive as I would like to be!" "*It's awful* that the Board of Directors knows I loused up that stock deal we almost made!" For self-condemnation never stems merely from your *observation* that you have done poorly on your job, with your wife, in your social life, or in any other aspect of your existence; it stems from your moralistic Belief, or conclusion, that *it's awful* that you failed in these respects.

Whenever you feel, at point C, again, the emotional Consequences of extreme anger, resentment, hostility, fury, vindictiveness, or some other feeling of hatred, you are telling yourself something like *"It's awful* that the lousy president of our company doesn't appreciate me enough!" *"It's awful* that my co-workers keep behaving stupidly or inefficiently!" *"It's awful* that my dratted wife is so undiscerning and insensitive!" *"It's awful* that those idiots on the Board of Directors think I loused up that big stock deal when I really didn't!" For, again, condemnation of others doesn't result from your *observation* that they have acted poorly or treated you unjustly. It results, instead, from your self-righteous, grandiose *Belief* that *it's awful* that they have not treated you the way they *should* have treated you.

Whenever you feel, at point C again, the dysfunctional Consequences of overwhelming frustration, inability to get moving, procrastination, irresponsible shirking, and similar manifestations of low frustration tolerance (or what is often called "laziness"), you are convincing yourself, something like, *"It's awful* that marriage is such a difficult state that I can't possibly live happily with my wife!" *"It's awful* that things are so arranged that it's impossible for me to be a truly efficient executive!" *"It's awful* that the Board of Directors keep seeing me as stupid when I'm really brilliant!" For condemnation of the world and its too, too hard conditions does not arise from your knowledge that things are imperfect and that life is rough. It stems, instead, from your whining, puerile Belief that *it's awful* that the world is often so grim and harsh and that it never, never *should* be.

Emotional disturbances, then, practically always arise from your unrealistic, exaggerated blaming—the blaming of yourself, of others, and of world conditions. When you behave neurotically, you overgeneralizingly flagellate persons and things, some of whose *aspects* you find undesirable. Instead of *wanting, wishing,* and *preferring* that these people and things have better characteristics, you *demand* and *dictate* that they immediately and completely improve. And you endlessly convince yourself, "It's awful, it's awful, it's awful!" when these people and things do not magically, thoroughly, spontaneously alter.

"It hardly seems possible that *all* my emotional upsets result from my believing that something is truly awful."

It may not seem possible, but it still appears to be true that virtually every single time you feel truly upset, you are awfulizing.

"Mmm. Perhaps so. Anyway, assuming this is true, how can I stop doing so by merely using two magical words?"

You can't. There is no magic, as far as I know, in the universe. You can use—that is, vigorously believe in—two potent words, if you would quickly undo your awfulizing. But there's no magic about them."

"*What* words? I can hardly wait to hear!"

The two words I usually recommend are: "Tough shit!" If you really believe these words, and the basic philosophy for which they stand, you will instantly start to lose your extreme feelings of anxiety, depression, and shame and become emotionally unblocked.

"What do you mean by 'the basic philosophy for which they stand'?"

Merely that these words are a shorthand version of the longer philosophy, "Tough shit!—that's the way I behave: imperfectly. Now, I can accept that fact and practice behaving less imperfectly—for example, work at doing better on my job so that I later get the promotion I am not getting right now. But if I never act much more perfectly and never get the promotion I want, that's still only tough shit! It's not awful—merely very inconvenient. And I can find some way to be relatively happy even when I am still highly imperfect and am thereby very inconvenienced."

"Uh-mm. I see. And what is the longhanded philosophy I can convince myself of in order to quickly do away with my intense feelings of anger and resentment?"

The philosophy that says: "Tough shit!—that's the way the president of my company is: unappreciative of me. I'd better accept that grim reality, and see what I can do to encourage him to be more appreciative. But if I can't do anything, I can't: it's still tough shit! He's not a bastard for having this failing, of being unappreciative. He has the right to be wrong, even though I'll never like his being wrong about me; and I can either calmly stay in the organization and enjoy myself in spite of his lack of appreciation, or else I can calmly look for another job where the president may be more appreciative of me."

"I see. And I guess I can figure out the longhanded

philosophy that I could use to do away with feelings of low frustration tolerance."

Yes, you easily could. Let's see you take a stab at it right now.

"All right; let me see. 'Tough shit!—so marriage is a difficult state that makes it almost impossible for me to live very happily with my wife. If I stop foolishly convincing myself that it's awful *because* it's so difficult, I can probably reduce some of its difficulties and get along somewhat better with my wife. And if that proves to be utterly impossible, then it's still tough shit! I can always lead a rather happy life even if I decide to divorce her.' "

Right! You see how you can quickly zero in on the tough shit philosophy—and state or imply by it that nothing is sacred and nothing is awful. Your behavior, others' behavior, or the world's conditions merely often stink. So they stink! Why *shouldn't* they? Why is that terrible? Why can't you lead a pretty calm and happy existence even if you, other people, and the world don't improve?

"I'm beginning to see more clearly what you mean."

I'm glad you are. Not that you have to use the exact terminology that I usually recommend to most people. If the words "Tough shit!" seem öffensive to you, you can employ nicer-sounding variations, such as "That's tough!" or "Too bad!" or "Tough titty!" Or you can even use the single word, "Tough!" or some other variation of your own.

The exact words do not greatly matter, but the *idea* does. For it is *not awful, horrible,* or *catastrophic* if you don't get promoted, if you are not as efficient as you'd like to be, if your wife doesn't love you as much as she previously did, or if the Board of Directors blames you for making a poor stock deal. You may easily, because you are a crooked-thinking human, believe, convince yourself, and be dogmatically certain that it *is* awful; and you may pigheadedly hold onto this idea forever. But *thinking* it is awful won't *make* it so or *prove* it so. It will merely, in most instances, make you *feel* that it is awful, and thereby emotionally upset you.

There is, in other words, a reasonably objective reality around you; and it does have some hard-headed advantages and disadvantages. Breaking your leg just before you are about to take a trip to Europe *may* turn out to be a wonderful occurrence. For you may, with a broken leg, be given special privileges by the airlines, encourage your wife to wait on you hand and foot, avoid boring sightseeing trips that you would otherwise have felt obliged to make, and so on. But *the chances are* that breaking your leg, in such circumstances, will be more unfortunate than fortunate and that you would enjoy yourself more in Europe with two good legs than with one incapacitated one. The Activating Events that happen to you, at point A, *do* partly influence your life; and it is normally far nicer if they influence it favorably than unfavorably. Consequently, it's damned *inconvenient* when these events are negative; but it's hardly *awful*.

So when, after something unfortunate happens (or is in danger of happening) at point A, you vigorously and quickly convince yourself, "Tough shit!" "Too bad!" "Tough!" or some equivalent rational idea, you are, in the vast majority of cases, appropriately describing and reacting to reality. You are then not exaggerating, not overgeneralizing, not catastrophizing about the unpleasant aspects of that reality, but accurately acknowledging them, accepting them for what they are, and determinedly thinking, "O.K. So the world is rough. So that's the way it is right now. So I'd better accept the bad with the good. So that's life. Now what the devil do I do to make my existence a little less rough, a little less unfortunate? And how do I prevent myself from whining about its disadvantages, in order to give myself more time and energy to work at minimizing or removing them?"

A good many people fall into an easy trap when they think about combating the "awfulness" that they are foolishly attributing to the disadvantageous Activating Experiences that occur in their lives at point A. Instead of saying to themselves at point B, "Too bad!" or "Tough!" they cavalierly jump over to "So what?" This is a distortion and itself an overgeneralization, because it implies that it really doesn't matter at *all* whether they fail to get promoted, lose their wives' affection, have their co-workers interfere with their efficiency, or are severely blamed by their Boards of Directors. The hell it doesn't! As noted above, it doesn't matter *all-importantly* if you break your leg just before you leave on a European trip; but it *does* matter.

This is why I strongly advocate the "Tough shit!" form of interrupting your catastrophizing; and why I generally recommend the use of four-letter words, at least when you express them to yourself. For they are forceful, vigorous, and difficult to misconstrue. If, when your superior fails to recognize how hard you are working and only endorses your work half-heartedly, you sanely tell yourself "Too bad!" or "Tough!" instead of "It's awful!" you are clearly on the right track. But "Too bad!" is a little namby-pamby and can easily be followed by: "Well, I guess I'll just have to put up with this kind of crummy behavior by my superior. What else can I do?" Even "Tough!" once you say it to yourself, can easily be glossed over, and you can cavalierly forget about how tough it is and keep self-defeatingly tolerating conditions which you really don't have to tolerate.

"Tough shit!" has a considerably stronger and more motivating connotation. For it implies, first, that the Activating Event which is interfering with your efficient functioning or happiness, at point A, really is uncomfortable, unpleasant; and that you don't *want* it to continue. It implies, second, that this unpleasantness warrants concerted action on your part to change it—to convince your superior, for example, that you are a more valuable executive than he thinks you are.

It implies, third, that, if you cannot change the disadvantageous situation at point A right now, you'd better look around for alternatives that will help you change it later. Thus, you may not, for practical reasons, be able to leave your firm or get transferred to a new department in it at present; but, if your supervisor is prejudiced against you and is giving you a hard time, you may well be able to plot and scheme to leave your firm or get transferred to a new department in the future.

"Tough shit!" implies, fourth, that things are rather rough on you at present but that there is no reason that they *should not* or *must not* be. It is tough that the world in general really doesn't give a fig about you and probably never will; and it is tough that certain people in the world, such as your wife, who may care for you more than others do, still only care for you intermittently, occasionally, and with many lapses of courtesy and consideration. But that's the way the world and the people who love you are! No one promised you a rose garden; and if they did, they were very wrong. Tough!

It implies, finally, that, if all your efforts to change the unsatisfactory Activating Events that you are experiencing at point A prove either temporarily or permanently to be of no avail, and if you are almost certain to keep experiencing this unpleasant stimulus, it is still only tough but *not* awful, horrible, terrible. You *can* stand it; you *can* continue to put up with it; you *don't* have to think that the world will come to an end or that you cannot possibly be happy in any way because of it. What happens, at point A, does cause you *some* degree of pain and discomfort; but it just about never forces you to experience *all* pain and *no* pleasure.

Although I do not, therefore, insist upon, I do heartily endorse your employment of various appropriate four-letter (and longer!) expletives. Not that these cannot be misused or abused. They can be. If, for example, when your superior refuses to recognize your value to the company or to see that you get a well-deserved promotion, you first tell yourself, "That's awful! I can't stand it!" and if you wisely decide to contradict this nonsense you are believing, you may then convince yourself, "Fuck it! It doesn't really matter what he thinks of me." But that is wrong, and is the same kind of mistaken "So what?" attitude that I questioned a few paragraphs back. For it *does* matter, at least to some extent, what he thinks of your work and of you; and to tell yourself "Fuck it!" is to overgeneralize in an indiscriminating and noninsightful way.

Similarly, if under the same conditions, you were to say to yourself, about your superior's refusing to recognize your value to the company, "Screw him!" that would be a poor use of expletives. For "Screw him!" doesn't exactly mean, "I don't agree with his estimation of my work and me, therefore I'll stick with my own opinion of how I am doing and will try to show him he is wrong about me or will look for some other position." It also means, "He is quite wrong about my work; and he is a lousy bastard for *being* wrong. He *shouldn't* unfairly view me the way he does!"

"Screw him!" "Fuck it!" and similar expletives may therefore, at least temporarily, reduce your inappropriate feelings of worthlessness—that is, your belief that you are a thorough slob if he doesn't like your work. But these terms "help you" at the expense of encouraging you to be grandiose and hostile—and thereby, in all probability, to get yourself into needless other difficulties (with your supervisor and others) as a concomitant of reducing (or sidetracking yourself from) your self-deprecation.

You could achieve a much better solution to this problem by vigorously convincing yourself, instead of "Screw him!", "Screw his *views* of me!" Then you would be more accurately showing yourself that he is a fallible human being, and not a lousy bastard, and that you don't have to agree with some of his fallible judgments, particularly his judgment of you and your work.

Four-letter words, then, for all their usefulness, would better be appropriately and accurately—and not sloppily—employed. This is true whether you say them to yourself or overtly express them to others. For, when efficiently used, they can be beneficial in both respects.

If you are now or intend in the near future to become a top executive, you'd better be forthright, direct, explicit, and forceful in much of the language you use with your associates. For if you continually say, "Please, Mr. President, do you mind if I make a suggestion?" or "Look, John, I am terribly upset by the fact that you keep coming in late almost every day," your superiors, peers, and subordinates may think you're a nice guy and a real gentleman; but they're also going to tend to believe you are pretty weak and that they can get away with all kinds of important things.

On the other hand, if you commonly say to your associates things like, "You know, Mr. President, I have a fucking good suggestion to make!" or "Look, John, I think your coming in late almost every day is a shitty thing for you to do to the rest of us who have to cover for you," your fellow workers are more likely to give a firmer meaning to your words and to take your ideas and comments seriously.

This does not mean, as you may well imagine, that you should unselectively employ so-called gutter language. If the chairman of your Board of Directors happens to be a stiff-necked Mormon or Orthodox Jew who seems unable to take even the mildest expletive, you'd better not say, "I've really been getting on the ass of those lazy cunts in the secretarial pool, and boy are they farting out more work these days!" And don't enthusiastically recite in his presence the latest dirty joke you learned from your golf companions. Or if the main buyers of your product are little old ladies who run gift shoppes, you don't encourage your sales representatives to speak to them in barroom language. But there are many instances, especially when you are speaking to certain kinds of people in your company, when you would be more effective using other four-letter words than *love*. And you'd better selectively note these instances and adapt your language accordingly.

Back to the main point in this chapter. Using shorthand statements, either to yourself or others, has its distinct limitations: for you thereby tend to gloss over some of the important ingredients of your intra- or intercommunications. Such shorthand declarations, moreover, can encourage glib-seeming acceptance (but actual nonacceptance) of a significant point. You can, for example, say to yourself, "Oh, well, that's the way it is," when things go wrong in your life. And you can then *think* that you are convincing yourself, "I tried everything I could possibly do to show our executive vice president that we would be much better off buying a lot of materials now, when the market is low, rather than waiting until the fall, when prices are almost bound to rise considerably. But unfortunately my best efforts failed and there's nothing else I can do in this respect. Oh, well, that's the way it is. I'll just have to accept the fact that we'll make less profit this year than we otherwise would have made had I been able to convince him."

Actually, however, you may mean: "What a stubborn person our executive vice president is! It's too difficult talking to him, so why should I try? Even though I haven't told him my idea about how much better off we'd be buying a lot of materials now, when the market is low, I'm sure he'd never go along with that idea, and he'd probably hate my guts for being so smart as to suggest it. Oh, well, that's the way it is. I might as well give up and let him be as goddamned stubborn and stupid as he is!" With this kind of "rational" thinking you may cop out too easily and stop trying to influence the vice president.

So watch your shorthand declarations! Don't think that, just because your self-sentences are short and curt, they are necessarily effective. Maybe they are and maybe they aren't. *Which* self-statements are you using? And *what* results are they effectuating?

Nonetheless, it can still generally be said that in the realm of emotional disturbance almost all the major upsets that you experience can be traced to your employing, in some level and in some way, the crazy belief, "It's awful!" And almost all these upsets can be quickly interrupted with the challenging and counterattacking beliefs, "Tough shit!" "Too bad!" "That's tough!" et cetera. Why not, appropriately and experimentally, try this kind of anti-awfulizing and anti-catastrophizing shorthand to see how unupsettable you can make yourself? What have you got to lose?

12 More instant attacks on emotional upsets

The beauty of the "Tough shit!" attack on any of your emotional upsets is that it really can work instantly and, if used consistently, it has profound philosophic effects on your thinking and your living. For if you are anxious and depressed, if you are hostile and resentful, and if you are procrastinating and "lazy," and if you directly and vigorously track down your awfulizing Beliefs and vehemently attack them, you will almost always feel a great sense of release, relief, and structural reorganization. If you truly *believe*, even temporarily, that it *is* tough shit if you fail, if others treat you inconsiderately, and if the world is rough, you will immediately lose your anxiety, hatred, and low frustration tol-

erance. And, after going through this process many
times, you will have difficulty in restoring these self-
defeating feelings, even though the Activating Events of
your life, at point A, continue to be exceptionally
difficult.

There are some other instant attacks that you can
make on your disturbed feelings, though they may take
a longer period of time to lead to good and lasting results. The first of these is rational-emotive imagery. Part
of the imaging technique was invented many years ago
by H. Bernheim and other pioneers in the field of hyp-
nosis and by Emile Coué and his fellow pioneers in the
field of auto-suggestion. It has been pushed in more recent years by Dorothea Brande, Robert Assaglioli, Nor-
man Vincent Peale, Maxwell Maltz, and other writers
and therapists who call it by various names, such as positive thinking and imaging.

In its original version, imaging or positive thinking
consists of the individual's interrupting his negative
thinking—such as his picturing himself as a failure, an
incompetent, or a worthless slob—and instead deliberately picturing himself as a person who succeeds, who
does things very well, or who is good and noble. I have
used this method many times with my clients and I have
no doubt that it is often effective and that those who consistently employ it tend to give up the idea that they can't
succeed and are no good and replace it with the belief
that they can succeed and are good persons.

There are several important limitations with this
method of positive thinking: (1) It covers up, rather

than truly replaces, the individual's concept of himself as a failure and a louse. It is quite possible for him to image himself as a success and a lovely person and yet, underlyingly, *also* see himself as a no-goodnik. (2) It falsely emphasizes success as a measure of human goodness. It essentially teaches the person, in most instances, "You *can* do well, and *therefore* you are not a turd. But if at any time you start doing consistently poorly again, you sink back to turdhood!" (3) It is not philosophically depth-centered or restructuring. It fails to show the emotionally upset individual that he really can *not* be, except by arbitrary definition in his own head, a worthless individual; that he doesn't *have* to prove himself in any way (though it is lovely if he changes some of his disadvantageous traits); and that *all* self-rating, or judging an individual in a total or global manner, is illegitimate and ultimately self-defeating. (4) It is palliative. Since the person who uses positive thinking almost always retains the fundamental philosophy that he *would* be pretty worthless if he failed or was disapproved by others, he has to keep imaging himself as succeeding and being loved. He rarely gets to the point where he *automatically* accepts himself as a fallible human being, *whether or not* he succeeds or is approved by others.

Because of its intrinsic limitations, the usual superficial and palliative forms of positive thinking have been replaced in recent years by a number of outstanding psychotherapists, including Joseph Cautela, Arnold Lazarus, and Maxie C. Maultsby, Jr. Dr. Maultsby and I, in a series of papers, have particularly emphasized the use of rational-emotive imagery, which goes far beyond positive thinking and which can be quickly taught to almost any troubled individual.

You may employ rational-emotive imagery in the following manner. Whenever you strongly believe you can't do something and that's awful and there is something rotten about you for not being able to do it, make a concerted effort to imagine or image in your head that (1) you *are* able to do and are actually doing that thing and (2) when you are so far failing at it, that you are not a louse, that it is too bad that you are failing, but that no horrible consequences will result from your failing at it.

The first part of this technique of rational-emotive imagery is the same as the usual form of positive thinking. Instead of picturing yourself—as you often have unwittingly trained yourself to do—as *not* being able to do something (such as speak adequately in public or present yourself to the president of your organization) you practice picturing yourself as being able to do this thing quite adequately. If you continue this kind of positive thinking, you will frequently be able to do what you think you cannot do, after awhile to do it very well, and after a longer period of time, to assume automatically that you can do it and keep trying it, without anxiety and depression, whenever the chance arises to perform it. Negative thinking is such a normal and natural—though unhealthy— part of human existence that practicing positive thinking will often minimize or practically eliminate it and will help make you much more effective in many different ways.

It is the second part of rational-emotive imagery, however, which is more important and unique to Rational Sensitivity. For no matter how beautifully and how often you picture yourself succeeding at, say, public speaking, there are times when you are bound to fail. You are, as I keep insisting, human rather than superhuman; and all humans inevitably fail. Therefore, to try to teach yourself techniques by which you will never, or even very rarely, fail is utopian; you are most unlikely to succeed at never failing.

Rational Sensitivity, however, takes the viewpoint that *nothing*—yes, *nothing*—is sacred or all-important, including consistent and profound failing. Many things, including many successes, are quite important—meaning that performing adequately or outstandingly will add significantly to your satisfactions. So by all means try to do these kinds of things well—for enjoyment, not for self-proving.

But when you fail, you fail. Tough! But hardly awful, horrible, or catastrophic! That is what Rational Sensitivity teaches; and that is what you can effectively teach yourself through persistent rational-emotive imaging. In a marathon weekend of rational encounter which I led a while ago with a group of individuals, several of whom were business executives and proprietors, one thirty-five-year-old vice president kept angering himself at his fellow officers in his company and at many of the other executives with whom he had to keep dealing. "But they *are* shits!" he kept reiterating to the marathon group. "They're impossibly stupid! And they keep acting viciously and trying to do me in. Of course I hate them! I'm glad I do!"

Under group questioning, however, this vice president admitted that he had a perpetual pain in his gut (and an ulcer to go with it), that he lost a good deal of business for his company by making himself enraged at some of its customers, and that, in spite of his hard work and his financial genius, his company might soon have to get rid of him if he kept behaving this childishly. So the group tried to convince him that he didn't have to hate anyone, either inside or outside his firm, and that he could legitimately feel exceptionally displeased with their *behavior* but didn't have to put *them* down in his head. He theoretically agreed with the group, but then said: "All right. But how can I actually *do* what you are telling me I'd better do? *How* do I change my philosophy and stop angering myself?"

After some discussion of how he could keep contradicting and Disputing—at point D—his irrational Belief —at point B—that others *should and must* act intelligently and nonvindictively, I gave him this rational-emotive imagery homework assignment: "Every day, for at least the next few weeks, put aside five minutes to practice the following imagery. Picture yourself, as vividly as you can, talking with some of the people in your own organization or in other firms who you think keep acting stupidly and nastily. See, in your imagination, exactly what they are doing and saying that you heartily disapprove of. See them doing precisely what they ordinarily do that you frequently upset yourself about. Then picture yourself calmly listening to them, noting to yourself that they are behaving stupidly and badly, and convincing yourself, 'Tough shit! That's the way they are!

They've always been like that, and they probably will pretty much continue to be that way. Tough!' Then picture yourself calmly continuing to listen to them, accepting them with their crummy traits, and only being displeased but not angry or otherwise upset. Do you get that picture you are to vividly rehearse for at least five minutes every day? They are doing exactly what you object to their doing—but you are calmly thinking about what they are doing and refusing to incense yourself about it. Then you are, further, dealing with them sensibly and making the best arrangements that you can make with them. No excuses, now! At least five minutes a day of rehearsing—vividly imagining in your head—their poor behavior, how you can think sanely about it, and what you can do to cope with it successfully."

This vice president took the rational-emotive imagery homework assignment, and reported back to the marathon reunion (which routinely is scheduled several weeks after we give a marathon weekend of rational encounter at the Institute for Advanced Study in Rational Psychotherapy) that he had, with few exceptions, carried out this assignment for five minutes a day for several weeks. "At first," he said, "I just did it routinely and it worked moderately well. That is to say, I got a little less upset about the stupid and negative behavior of others. But then, as I saw that it really was working, I did it with much more vigor and vividness, and soon I really began to see people differently. I fully began to realize that they *are* fallible, and that *isn't* awful. I became particularly good at writing scripts in my head picturing myself calmly reacting to them no matter *how* poorly they behaved; and I convinced myself that I *could* act that way. Soon I was almost always following out my pictured script. And now only occasionally, with great provocation, do I seem to deviate from it. My associates at work are amazed at the change in me; and several of our customers have remarked on it to me or to other officers in our firm. This is now really becoming a part of me! I not only *know* that I can act in a grown-up manner when others around me act like children, I also see exactly why I'd better react this way. I'd say that my entire outlook on life is changing!"

In many other ways, rational-emotive imagery can be used to overcome your actual or potential upsets. Before you fail at some task, like writing a good report for example, you can image yourself refusing to belabor yourself if you fail. And when you actually write the report and it turns out to be mediocre, you can see yourself handing it in, having it disapproved, not liking this disapproval, but still not feeling destroyed, hurt, or worthless about it. Then you can picture youself (1) writing better reports in the future and (2) accepting your ineptitude gracefully when you happen to write a poor one.

There are very few potentially disturbing Activating Events to which rational-emotive imagery cannot be successfully applied. You can vividly envision yourself making difficult decisions, taking notable risks, getting through social affairs unperturbably, dealing with your mate's and your children's inanities and insanities, accepting sexual failure if and when it occurs, and philosophically acclimating yourself to virtually any kind of difficulty or hassle that is likely to come along. By all means, convince yourself, by the steady use of rational-emotive imagery, that you *can* do many things you often think you can't do. But go far beyond this, and show yourself that, even when you miserably fail, it is still not horrible and you are never an awful person. Once you work at viewing yourself with equanimity even when you indubitably fail in some manner, you will normally continue to practice that performance and eventually probably succeed. But success, again, is never *all*-important; it is merely nice, fortunate, and important. If rational-imagery can help teach you that, it will do you one of the best services that anything has ever done you in your entire life.

Another simple, direct, and instantly applicable technique of helping you with your emotional problems—especially those of lateness, procrastination, inertia, and general goofing—is that of setting yourself reinforcement schedules. This method basically goes back to the famous psychologist, B. F. Skinner, who did a great deal of work with reinforcement schedules with animals and humans, and proved conclusively that if an individual (or a pigeon) is rewarded every time he does a certain act and is penalized (or at least, deprived) every time he does not do it, his behavior may change enormously, so that he keeps "naturally" and spontaneously performing the reinforced act. A number of behavior therapists, particularly Lloyd Homme and Arnold Lazarus, have utilized this principle by combining it with D. Premack's theory of reinforcement.

Premack found that the reinforcer that will help an individual to change his behavior need not be a primary

reinforcer—such as food, water, or sex. It may also be almost any kind of secondary reinforcer—such as any act
that the individual considers to be easy and satisfying.
Homme discovered that even young children can be
asked what activities they find rewarding and will answer
that they like walking around the room, talking to others,
or yelling. Then, if the teacher wants them to pay attention to classroom activities for, say, ten minutes—an activity that the children often do not find very easy—she
can say to them, "Look, children. If you will only pay attention for the next ten minutes, *then* I shall be happy to
let you walk around the room, talk to others, or yell."
Rewarding the children in this manner frequently enables
them to pay better attention than trying to get them to do
so with other teaching methods.

You can employ self-reinforcement schedules to induce yourself to perform almost any kind of difficult or
disciplined activity. Thus, if you are having trouble writing business reports and keep avoiding doing so, you can
say to yourself: "Enough of that procrastination. Let me
see what I really enjoy doing and easily do almost every
day in the week. Mmm. Eating. Listening to music. Talking to my friends. Playing golf. All right. I will only permit myself, hereafter, to have a good dinner *after* I have
already spent at least two hours a day working on my reports. And no nonsense about it! At least two hours a
day working on my reports—or no dinner!"

Similarly, you can schedule yourself to do all kinds of
seemingly onerous tasks—such as dieting, refraining
from smoking, speaking to your boss about a raise, getting the things on and in your desk in order, outlining a

new sales campaign—by refusing to permit yourself to do some easy, highly enjoyable thing unless and until you do the difficult one. Like the assistant manager of a moderately large manufacturing concern who came to one of the Executive Workshops held by the Institute for Rational Living. "How," he asked me and the group of assembled executives, "can I get myself to answer the letters of complaint that I receive from time to time? Hell, I must have about thirty of them piled up in my drawer right now—some of which I've had there for months. And, you know how it is. First they complain. Then they complain that their complaint hasn't been answered. Then they complain that their first two letters haven't been replied to. And so on, almost ad infinitum! What the devil can I do?"

We tried several methods with this individual. We showed him that, if he did answer the original complaint, and he even answered it poorly and without satisfying the complainant, this would hardly make him a horrible person. It would only mean that he did a poor job; or, perhaps, that *no* answer would satisfy this particular person. But in either event, he, a whole human being, would hardly be a louse.

We showed him, secondly, that he had somewhat typical low frustration tolerance, and kept telling himself, foolishly: "It's a hell of a pain in the ass to answer these letters. It's not really my job anyhow, since it has been unfairly turned over to me by the general manager. Why should I have to do what is really supposed to be *his* work? And answering letters like this is not merely hard, it's *too* hard, and I shouldn't have to do anything so hard! I think I'll just let the blasted letters pile up, to see if I and everyone else just can't forget about them."

We showed him how to Dispute these irrational ideas by asking himself: "Why should I *not* have to do this onerous task, even though it's unfair for the general manager to turn it over to me? Who am I to demand absolute fairness in the world? And why, although it's hard to reply to these kinds of letters, is it *too* hard? Isn't it much harder for me *not* to answer them, and merely create additional work for myself? Will the writers of the letters really forget about them if I let them pile up? Will that kind of evasive behavior truly do me any but ephemeral good?"

While getting him to challenge his basic irrational philosophy in these ways, the workshop group also suggested a simple self-reinforcing schedule. They induced this avoidant executive to give up intercourse with his wife until he was caught up, and remained caught up, with his answers to the complaints. Since he was a highly sexed individual and thoroughly enjoyed copulating with his wife, it took only a few days for him to answer all the complaining letters on hand; and for the next six months —as he later informed me—there never was a single day when he did not immediately answer any complaint that was received. Meanwhile, his sexual prowess kept up with his letter-writing prowess, and he and his wife had a ball! As he wrote in a follow-up letter to me: "I'm not sure whether I am more grateful to you and the workshop group for the enormously less anxiety and greater relaxation I now feel because the letters are no longer hanging over my head or for the great marital sex which my new patterns of work have helped me enjoy. I never realized, when I first came to your executive workshop, that the results I might derive would be so goddamned sexy! But I'm not complaining!"

Self-reinforcement schedules may be effectively employed in a large variety of ways. Within the past few weeks, I have helped some of my clients write reports, make up sales plans, attend social gatherings, be affectionate with their family members, redecorate their offices, give up smoking, and do a host of other tasks which they considered too difficult—by figuring out with them some kind of self-reinforcement schedule and monitoring them for a while in keeping to that schedule. Moreover, when I have used this method in conjunction with the "Tough shit!" and the rational-emotive imagery techniques outlined in this and the previous chapter, major restructurings of several individuals' basic personality structures have begun to occur. None of these techniques, used singly or together, is a panacea for all emotional problems. Nothing is! But when vigorously and persistently applied, they can help the individual go a long way in overcoming some of his deepest and longest-standing blockings.

Why not try them and see?

13 Rational Sensitivity
and the future

Rational Sensitivity has enormous possibilities—for your future and, very possibly, for the world's. For it is not only a method of quickly getting at the source of virtually all emotional problems and of temporarily and permanently resolving them. And it is not only a personal technique which you can employ for your own and your close associates' advantage. It is a way of life, a world view—which, if it were widely and consistently practiced, might well aid the minimizing of numerous societal ills, such as war, social injustice, ecological destruction, miseducation, and rampant superstition.

The rationally sensitized person is, of course, no arch-

179

angel; he continues to err in numerous indigenously human ways. But he is relevantly directed toward living and enjoying; he is humanistically absorbed in himself and his fellow men (and women); he is scientific and realistic; and he is therefore much less likely to foment individual and social disorganization than is the irrational, insensitized person. Although one of his major goals may be to realize himself as a competent executive, he does so in the light of human thought and feeling and is rationally self- *and* socially interested.

Rational Sensitivity means, in other words, that the individual who believes in and practices this philosophic orientation is highly sensitized

to himself and his survival and enjoyments;

to other human beings and their desires to live and be happy;

to short-range *and* long-range pleasures and pains;

to his own propensity to create his highly emotionalized feelings (at point C), about the Activating Events and Experiences he encounters (at point A), by actively thinking and valuing (at point B);

to the fact that practically all humans, including himself, are frequently needlessly disturbed;

to discriminating accurately between his rational, empirically centered and his irrational, magic-impelled beliefs;

to the difficulty of his (and others') changing basic thinking and emoting patterns;

to the possibility, nonetheless, of such radical change being effected;

to the desirability of continual work and practice, at

his own thinking and behaving patterns, in order to effect basic personality change.

If you would practice Rational Sensitivity, you may make good use of the brief, instantly applicable methods outlined in the previous two chapters. But you can also, especially when the going is rough, employ the long-handed version of RS and systematically explore and think through the A-B-C's of emotional disturbance. One practical means of doing this is to use steadily, at least for a period of time, the Homework Reports which are distributed to clients and to others by the Institute for Advanced Study in Rational Psychotherapy. This two-page report is printed on pages 182-185.

On page one of the Homework Report, you can list your undesirable emotional feelings, undesirable actions or habits, and irrational ideas or philosophies—particularly those which troubled you during the past week or two. You then can fill in the amount of work you did on these feelings, habits, and philosophies, and the results of this work. By filling in this part of the form, you have available a running account, from week to week, of how you are feeling and doing and how you are working to feel and perform more satisfactorily.

On page two of the Homework Report, you first have the heart of the longhanded versions of the Rational Sensitivity process: the A-B-C-D-and-E's which show you precisely how upset you are, what happened before you became upset, what your rational and irrational Beliefs are which are creating the upsetness, how you can vigorously and consistently Dispute your irrational Beliefs, what cognitive Effects you are likely to get as a

HOMEWORK REPORT

Consultation Center

Institute for Advanced Study in Rational Psychotherapy

45 East 65th Street, New York, N.Y. 10021 / (212) LEhigh 5-0822

Name .... Date .... Therapist ....

Instructions: Please draw a circle around the number in front of those feelings listed in the first column that troubled you *most* during the period since your last therapy session. Then, in the *second* column, indicate the amount of work you did on each circled item; and, in the *third* column, the results of the work you did.

	Amount of Work Done			Results of Work		
	Much	Some	Little or none	Good	Fair	Poor
Undesirable Emotional Feelings						
1a Anger or great irritability	1b			1c		
2a Anxiety, severe worry, or fear	2b			2c		
3a Boredom or dullness	3b			3c		
4a Failure to achieve	4b			4c		
5a Frustration	5b			5c		
6a Guilt or self-condemnation	6b			6c		
7a Hopelessness or depression	7b			7c		
8a Great loneliness	8b			8c		
9a Helplessness	9b			9c		
10a Self-pity	10b			10c		
11a Uncontrollability	11b			11c		
12a Worthlessness or inferiority	12b			12c		
13a Other (specify)	13b			13c		
....						
Undesirable Actions or Habits						
14a Avoiding responsibility	14b			14c		
15a Acting unfairly to others	15b			15c		

16a	Being late to appointments	16b	....	16c	....
17a	Being undisciplined	17b	....	17c	....
18a	Demanding attention	18b	....	18c	....
19a	Physically attacking others	19b	....	19c	....
20a	Putting off important things	20b	....	20c	....
21a	Telling people off harshly	21b	....	21c	....
22a	Whining or crying	22b	....	22c	....
23a	Withdrawing from activity	23b	....	23c	....
24a	Overdrinking of alcohol	24b	....	24c	....
25a	Overeating	25b	....	25c	....
26a	Oversleeping	26b	....	26c	....
27a	Undersleeping	27b	....	27c	....
28a	Oversmoking	28b	....	28c	....
29a	Taking too many drugs or pills	29b	....	29c	....
30a	Other (specify)	30b	....	30c	....
	....		....		

Irrational Ideas or Philosophies

31a	People must love or approve of me	31b	....	31c	....
32a	Making mistakes is terrible	32b	....	32c	....
33a	People should be condemned for their wrongdoings	33b	....	33c	....
34a	It's terrible when things go wrong	34b	....	34c	....
35a	My emotions can't be controlled	35b	....	35c	....
36a	Threatening situations have to keep me terribly worried	36b	....	36c	....
37a	Self-discipline is too hard to achieve	37b	....	37c	....
38a	Bad effects of my childhood still have to control my life	38b	....	38c	....
39a	I can't stand the way certain people act	39b	....	39c	....
40a	Other (specify)	40b	....	40c	....
	....		....		

(please complete other side)

PLEASE PRINT! BE BRIEF AND LEGIBLE! ANSWER QUESTION C FIRST; THEN ANSWER THE OTHER QUESTIONS.

A. ACTIVATING EVENT you recently experienced about which you became upset or disturbed. (Examples: *"I went for a job interview." "My mate screamed at me."*) ....

rB. Rational BELIEF or idea you had about this Activating Event. (Examples: *"It would be unfortunate if I were rejected for the job." "How annoying to have my mate scream at me!"*) ....

iB. Irrational BELIEF or idea you had about this Activating Event. (Examples: *"It would be catastrophic if I were rejected for the job; I would be pretty worthless as a person." "I can't stand my mate's screaming; she is horrible for screaming at me!"*) ....

C. CONSEQUENCES of your irrational BELIEF (iB) about the Activating Event listed in Question A. State here the one most disturbing emotion, behavior, or CONSEQUENCE you experienced recently. (Examples: *"I was anxious." "I was hostile." "I had stomach pains."*) ....

D. DISPUTING, questioning, or challenging you can use to change your irrational BELIEF (iB). (Examples: *"Why would it be catastrophic and how would I become a worthless person if I were rejected for the job?" "Why can't I stand my mate's screaming and why is she horrible for screaming at me?"*) ....

cE. Cognitive EFFECT or answer you obtained from DISPUTING your irrational BELIEF (iB). Examples: *"It would not be catastrophic, but merely unfortunate, if I were rejected for the job; my giving a poor interview would not make me a worthless person." "Although I'll never like my mate's screaming, I can stand it; he or she is not horrible but merely a fallible person for screaming."*) ....

bE. Behavioral EFFECT or result of your DISPUTING your irrational BELIEF (iB). (Examples: *"I felt less anxious." "I felt less hostile to my mate." "My stomach pains vanished."*) ....

F. If you did not challenge your irrational BELIEF (iB), why did you not? ....

G. Activities you would most like to *stop* that you are now doing ....

H. Activities you would most like to *start* that you are not doing ....

I. Emotions and ideas you would most like to change ....

J. Specific homework assignment(s) given you by your therapist, your group, or yourself ....

K. What did you actually do to carry out the assignment(s)? ....

L. Check the item which describes how much you have worked, at your last homework assignment(s): .... (a) almost every day .... (b) several times a week .... (c) occasionally .... (d) hardly ever.

M. How many times in the past week have you specifically worked at changing and DISPUTING your irrational BELIEFS (iBs)? ....

N. What other things have you specifically done to change your irrational BELIEFS and your disturbed emotional CONSE-QUENCES? ....

O. Check the item which describes how much reading you have recently done of the material on rational-emotive therapy: .... (a) a considerable amount .... (b) a moderate amount .... (c) little or none.

P. Things you would now like to discuss most with your therapist or group ....

result of such Disputing, and what behavioral Effects you will finally tend to get after Disputing. Rational-emotive-therapy clients and other individuals who use this form usually discover that it enables them to zero in with amazing precision on virtually any emotional Consequence (C) which currently bothers them, to discover its presumed origin (A) in the outside world, to admit its true causation in their own Belief System (B), to Dispute it at D in a vigorous manner, and quite quickly, in most instances, to wind up with a new cognitive Effect (cE) and a new behavioral Effect (bE) which enables them to feel and act much better, and to have a reduced chance of upsetting themselves similarly in the future.

In training yourself to use questions A to E on the second page of the Homework Report, it is advisable for you to work with a rational-emotive therapist, counselor, client, or student. For this individual can particularly correct your form several times, show you how to discriminate accurately between your rational and irrational Beliefs, and encourage you to keep using the outline steadily until it is virtually a natural part of your thinking process. You may, of course, do this without anyone to help you and correct your form; but it is safer to have some supervision, especially at the beginning.

Questions F to P on the second page of the Homework Report help you check on your Disputing, set future emotional-behavioral goals, give yourself specific homework assignments, continue to Dispute your irrational Beliefs, and read some further rational-emotive material. If, therefore, you fill out the entire report regularly for a while, you are likely to use the Rational Sensitivity approach in a more concerted and consistent manner.

As a sample exercise, let us take a typical emotional problem and fill out part of the Homework Report in an attempt to solve it. Let us take a problem that has important individual and social repercussions and is particularly relevant today in the executive world: the problem of the individual who is a member of a group that is frequently discriminated against in business and organizational life.

Let us suppose, for example, that you are both a woman and Black, and that you are having great difficulty getting along in the executive world, and attaining the highest positions, because of the real prejudices that exist against you. Various firms will employ you and let you work adequately; but just as soon as it comes to giving you a truly topflight position, the higher-ups begin to tell themselves that (1) you are a female, and will very likely put your love life and family affairs before your organizational career; and (2) you are Black, and will therefore have certain people, in your own and other firms, prejudiced against you, and consequently will not be too effective at certain jobs. As a result, they only permit you to go so far and no farther in the executive hierarchy.

You fill out the Homework Report and, as the instructions state, you first answer question C: the one most disturbing emotion, behavior, or CONSEQUENCE you experienced recently. So you write in the C blank: "Anger and depression."

You then go back to A and fill in the ACTIVATING EVENT you recently experienced about which you became upset or disturbed. So you state: "I received a salary raise but my firm refused to promote me to the title of general manager."

Then you fill in the rational BELIEF or idea you had about this Activating Event: "How unfair! I think they discriminated against me, because I am a woman and am Black, and that is extremely unjust and unfortunate!"

Then you think about the irrational BELIEF or idea you had about this Activating Event. You finally come up with: "How awful! It's terrible for them to discriminate against me like that! The lousy bastards!"

You then go on to D, and start DISPUTING, questioning, and challenging your irrational BELIEF. You write in: (1) "Why is it awful?" (2) "What is the evidence that it's terrible for them to discriminate against me like that? Why shouldn't they?" (3) "How are they lousy bastards for doing that to me?"

You really DISPUTE your irrational Beliefs, quite vigorously and persistently, until you finally wind up with a cognitive EFFECT or answer: (1) "It's not awful; it's only exceptionally inconvenient!" (2) "There's no evidence that it's terrible for them to discriminate against me like that. It's only unfair, unjust, and very annoying. There's no reason they should not, ought not, must not discriminate in that fashion." (3) "They're not lousy bastards, but merely fallible human beings who are acting wrongly and inefficiently."

If you truly persist at DISPUTING and answering your own challenges in this fashion, you genuinely feel a behavioral EFFECT of this DISPUTING: (1) "No longer angry." (2) "Lost my depression." (3) "Calmly joined a Woman's Lib group and am looking for a suitable group that is fighting sanely against discriminating against Blacks."

This, of course, is an ideal way to tackle your problem of feeling depressed and angry about being discriminated against. Many times you will not counterattack your upset feelings in this effective manner, and you will only partially go after them, or do so in a manner that Disputes them in a logical and an illogical manner. Temporarily, therefore, you will either fail to feel undepressed and unangry; or you will feel so for a brief period of time; or you will defensively forget about the entire problem of discrimination; or you will adopt some other low-level solution. But you can always continue to work at better, more truly rational solutions; and you can keep sensitizing yourself to what you are feeling, how you are creating your needlessly upsetting emotions, how you can clearly see the difference between your rational and irrational Beliefs, what you can do to Dispute your irrational Beliefs, and how you can end up with new philosophies and radically different, healthier feelings and behavior.

In this manner, you will probably not only solve your personal problems, you are likely to help your society think about and possibly ameliorate some of its hangups, inefficiencies, and injustices. For the better you change your behavior, the more your social group tends to benefit. And the more you help it change its ways, the more you and your loved ones tend to live happily and self-fulfillingly. Individual and social interest, especially in the long run, are not mutually incompatible; they are very much intertwined. The executive who helps himself also tends to help his organization, his fellow workers, his family and friends, and his general society. Personal Rational Sensitivity usually also pays social dividends.

What, in today's world, could be more relevant—meaning, more productive of human happiness? Rational still means leading to *human* well-being and fulfillment. Rational Sensitivity means the process and the practice of being sensitized to *that* goal.

On your mark . . . !

About the Author

Albert Ellis, born in Pittsburgh and reared in New York City, holds a bachelor's degree from the City College of New York and M.A. and Ph.D. degrees in Clinical Psychology from Columbia University. He has an appointment as Adjunct Professor of Psychology at Rutgers University and at United States International University. He served as Chief Psychologist of the New Jersey State Diagnostic Center and later as Chief Psychologist of the New Jersey Department of Institutions and Agencies; also as a Consultant in Clinical Psychology to the New York City Board of Education and to the Veterans Administration. He currently holds the position of Executive Director of the Institute for Rational Living and of the Institute for Rational-Emotive Therapy. He has practiced psychotherapy and marriage and family counseling, as well as sex therapy, for over thirty years and continues this practice at the Consultation Center of the Institute for Rational-Emotive Therapy in New York City.

A Fellow of the American Psychological Association, Dr. Ellis has served as President of its Division of Consulting Psychology and a member of its Council of Representatives. He is a Fellow (and Past President) of the Society for the Scientific Study of Sex; and a Fellow of the American Association of Marriage and Family Counselors, the American Orthopsychiatric Association, the American Sociological Association, the American Association for Applied Anthropology, and the American Association for the Advancement of Science. The American Association of Sex Educators, Counselors, and Therapists has qualified him as a Certified Sex Educator and a Certified Sex Therapist; and the American Association of Marriage and Family Counselors has appointed him an Approved Supervisor.

Dr. Ellis has also served as Vice President of the American Academy of Psychotherapists; Chairman of the Marriage Counseling Section of the National Council on Family Relations; and an Executive Committee Member of the Divisions of Psychotherapy and of Humanistic Psychology of the American Psychological Association, and of the New York Society of Clinical Psychologists. Several professional societies have honored him; and he holds the Humanist of the Year Award of the American Humanist Association, the Distinguished Professional Psychologist Award of the Division of Psychotherapy of the American Psychological Association, and the Distinguished Leadership Award of the American Association of Sex Educators, Counselors, and Therapists.

Dr. Ellis has served as Consulting or Associate Editor of many professional journals, including the *Journal of Marriage and the Family*, the *International Journal of Sexology, Existential Psychiatry*, the *Journal of Marriage and Family Counseling*, the *Journal of Contemporary Psychotherapy*, the *Journal of Individual Psychology*, the *Journal of Sex Research, Rational Living, Voices: the Art and Science of Psychotherapy*, and *Cognitive Therapy and Research*. He has published over five hundred papers in psychological, psychiatric, and sociological journals and anthologies. He has authored or edited more than forty books and monographs, including *Sex Without Guilt, How to Live with a "Neurotic," The Art and Science of Love, Reason and Emotion in Psychotherapy, How to Live With–and Without–Anger, Sex and the Liberated Man, Humanistic Psychotherapy: the Rational-Emotive Approach, A New Guide to Rational Living, Overcoming Procrastination, Handbook of Rational-Emotive Therapy,* and *Brief Psychotherapy in Medical and Health Practice*.